WRITERS AND THEIR WORK

ISOBEL ARMSTRONG
General Editor

THOMAS HARDY

HARDY WITHOUT EMMA IN LONDON, CIRCA 1900

a detail from the painting *First Night at a Theatre* by Alfred Stevens
by permission of the Thomas Hardy Memorial Collection, Dorset County Museum, Dorchester

WW

THOMAS HARDY

Peter Widdowson

Second Edition

NORTHCOTE

BRITISH COUNCIL

ATLANTIC
PUBLISHERS & DISTRIBUTORS (P) LTD

This edition is published by
ATLANTIC
PUBLISHERS & DISTRIBUTORS (P) LTD
7/22, Ansari Road, Darya Ganj, New Delhi-110 002
Tel: 40775252, 23273880, 23275880, 23280451; Fax: +91-11-23285873
E-mail: orders@atlanticbooks.com; Web: www.atlanticbooks.com

By arrangement with
Northcote House Publishers Ltd
Horndon House, Horndon, Tavistock, Devon, PL19 9NQ,
United Kingdom. (T)+44(0)1822 810066; (F)+44(0)1822 810034
(E) northcote.house@virgin.net and (W) www.northcotehouse.co.uk
The *Writers and their Work* series is published in association with the British Council.

Second edition 2007
First Indian Reprint 2010
First published in 1996 by Northcote House Publishers Ltd

ISBN 978-81-269-1298-8

British Library Cataloguing-in-Publication Data
A catalogue record for this book is available from the British Library

Typeset by PDQ Typesetting, Newcastle-under-Lyme
Printed in India at Nice Printing Press, A-33/3A, Site-IV,
Industrial Area, Sahibabad, Ghaziabad, U.P.

For Philip Martin

Contents

Acknowledgements

There seems to be a limit to what one can find new to say in one lifetime about any individual writer, and so some of what appears in the following study represents a refashioning of other work of mine on Hardy: in particular, on his fiction, *Hardy in History: A Study in Literary Sociology* (Routledge, 1989), and, on his poetry, the Introduction and Critical Commentary in *Thomas Hardy's Selected Poetry and Non-Fictional Prose* (Macmillan, 1996). I am indebted to Macmillan Press Ltd. (now Palgrave Macmillan) for the original permission to reprint the prose passages and seven complete poems by Hardy included here. For this new second edition, I have added a 'Postscript: Hardy from Page to Screen', offering a brief commentary on film and TV adaptations of his novels. For this, I have again drawn on much longer essays/chapters in my own previously published work: the Routledge volume cited above; *On Thomas Hardy: Late Essays and Earlier* (Macmillan, 1998); 'Thomas Hardy at the End of Two Centuries: From Page to Screen' in Tim Dolin and Peter Widdowson (eds.), *Thomas Hardy and Contemporary Literary Studies* (Palgrave Macmillan, 2004); 'The Silent Era: Thomas Hardy Goes Way Down East', in Terence Wright (ed.), *Thomas Hardy on Screen* (Cambridge University Press, 2005).

My thanks to Isobel Armstrong for supportive and fine-tuned comments on the original draft of the book; to my colleagues at the University of Gloucestershire – and in particular, Philip Martin, my Head of School at that time – for letting me get on with it; and to Jane and Tom, as always, for putting up with it.

Biographical Outline

1840	Thomas Hardy born on 2 June at Higher Bockhampton, near Dorchester, Dorset.
1848	'The Year of Revolutions' across Europe.
1848–56	Attends the village school, then transfers to a school in Dorchester.
1853–6	The Crimean War.
1856–62	Articled to Dorchester architect, John Hicks. Earliest poem, 'Domicilium', written between 1857 and 1860 (reproduced in Florence Emily Hardy's *The Life of Thomas Hardy*: see Select Bibliography).
1862–7	In London, working as an assistant to architect, Arthur Blomfield. Continues to write poetry.
1867–70	Returns to Dorchester. Works for Hicks, and then for his successor, Crickmay, in Weymouth. Starts first 'lost' novel, *The Poor Man and the Lady*. Completes draft 1868; decides not to publish it. Begins *Desperate Remedies*.
1870	Is sent by Crickmay to St Juliot, Cornwall, where he meets his future first wife, Emma Lavinia Gifford.
1871	*Desperate Remedies*, first published novel.
1872	*Under the Greenwood Tree*.
1873	*A Pair of Blue Eyes*.
1874	Marries Emma Gifford. *Far from the Madding Crowd* published: first major success. Decides to give up architecture and write fiction full-time.
1876	*The Hand of Ethelberta*.
1878	*The Return of the Native*. Moves to London.
1880	Publishes *The Trumpet-Major*. Serious illness while writing *A Laodicean* (published 1881).

1882	*Two on a Tower.*
1885	Moves into Max Gate, the house he builds outside Dorchester.
1886	*The Mayor of Casterbridge.*
1887	*The Woodlanders.*
1891	Publication of *Tess of the d'Urbervilles* creates a furore.
1892–4	Father dies (1892); relations with Emma deteriorate (especially during the writing of *Jude the Obscure*); 'love affair' with Florence Henniker.
1896	Publication of *Jude the Obscure* produces scandalized response. Resolves to give up novel-writing.
1897	*The Well-Beloved* published in book form (written after *Tess*; serial version, 1892).
1897–8	Preparing poems for first volume of poetry, *Wessex Poems* (published 1898).
1899–1902	The Boer War in South Africa. Queen Victoria dies in 1901.
1902	*Poems of the Past and the Present* (postdated; it appeared in Nov. 1901); begins writing his huge epic-drama in verse, *The Dynasts.*
1904	First two parts of *The Dynasts* published (subsequent parts in 1906, 1908). His mother dies.
1909	*Time's Laughingstocks and Other Verses* published.
1910	Awarded the Order of Merit and the freedom of Dorchester. Edward VII dies; George V becomes king.
1912	Final revision of his novels for the 'Wessex Edition'. Florence Emily Dugdale, future second wife, already acting as his assistant. Wife, Emma, dies suddenly in November.
1913	In March, makes 'pilgrimage' to scenes of early romance with Emma in Cornwall. Writes many of 'Poems of 1912–13'.
1914–18	The First World War.
1914	In February marries second wife, Florence Emily. *Satires of Circumstance, Lyrics and Reveries* published (includes 'Poems of 1912–13').
1915	His sister, Mary, dies.
1917	*Moments of Vision and Miscellaneous Verses* published.
1922	*Late Lyrics and Earlier* published (same year as T. S. Eliot's *The Waste Land* and James Joyce's *Ulysses*).

1925 *Human Shows, Far Phantasies, Songs and Trifles* published. Hardy composing 'Florence Emily Hardy's' *The Life of Thomas Hardy* throughout the mid-1920s.

1926 The General Strike in Great Britain.

1928 Dies, 11 January. Ashes buried in Poets' Corner, Westminster Abbey; his heart in Emma's grave in Stinsford churchyard, Dorset. *Winter Words in Various Moods and Metres* published posthumously, as is the first part of *The Life.*

Abbreviations and References

Page references to Hardy's novels, throughout, are to the Macmillan New Wessex editions of 1974–5 (since reprinted, with some variations in pagination). The standard collected editions of Hardy's shorter poems are: *Thomas Hardy: The Complete Poems,* ed. James Gibson (Basingstoke: Macmillan, 1976), and *The Complete Poetical Works of Thomas Hardy,* ed. Samuel Hynes, vols. i, ii, and iii (Oxford: Oxford University Press, 1982, 1984, 1985) – in both of which they are reprinted in the order in which they appeared in the original individual volumes of poetry. However, for ease of reference given the vast scale of Hardy's poetic production, all the poems referred to in the present study may be found in my *Thomas Hardy: Selected Poetry and Non-Fictional Prose* (with explanatory notes) (Basingstoke: Macmillan, 1996).

The following abbreviations are used for reference throughout the book.

DR	*Desperate Remedies* (1871), with intro. by C. J. P. Beatty (Basingstoke: Macmillan, 1975)
FMC	*Far from the Madding Crowd* (1874), with intro. by James Gibson (Basingstoke: Macmillan, 1974/5)
HE	*The Hand of Ethelberta* (1876), with intro. by Robert Gittings (Basingstoke: Macmillan, 1975)
HS	*Human Shows, Far Phantasies, Songs and Trifles* (London: Macmillan, 1925)
J.	*Jude the Obscure* (1896), with intro. by Terry Eagleton (Basingstoke: Macmillan, 1974)
L.	*A Laodicean* (1881), with intro. by Barbara Hardy (Basingstoke: Macmillan, 1975)

Life	Florence Emily Hardy, *The Life of Thomas Hardy, 1840–1928* (paperback edition, Basingstoke: Macmillan, 1975)
LLE	*Late Lyrics and Earlier with Many Other Verses* (London: Macmillan, 1922)
MC	*The Mayor of Casterbridge* (1886), with intro. by F. B. Pinion (Basingstoke: Macmillan, 1974/5)
MV	*Moments of Vision and Miscellaneous Verses* (London: Macmillan, 1917)
PBE	*A Pair of Blue Eyes* (1873), with intro. by Ronald Blythe (Basingstoke: Macmillan, 1975)
PPP	*Poems of the Past and the Present* (London: Harper & Brothers, 1901)
RN	*The Return of the Native* (1878), with intro. by J. C. S. Tremblett-Wood (Basingstoke: Macmillan, 1974/5)
SC	*Satires of Circumstance, Lyrics and Reveries* (London: Macmillan, 1914)
T.	*Tess of the d'Urbervilles* (1891), with intro. by James Gibson (Basingstoke: Macmillan, 1974/5)
TL	*Time's Laughingstocks and Other Verses* (London: Macmillan, 1909)
TM	*The Trumpet-Major* (1880), with intro. by Ray Evans (Basingstoke: Macmillan, 1974/5)
TT	*Two on a Tower* (1882), with intro. by F. B. Pinion (Basingstoke: Macmillan, 1975)
UGT	*Under the Greenwood Tree* (1872), with intro. by Geoffrey Grigson (Basingstoke: Macmillan, 1974)
W.	*The Woodlanders* (1887), with intro. by F. B. Pinion (Basingstoke: Macmillan, 1974/5)
WB	*The Well-Beloved* (1897), with intro. by J. Hillis Miller (Basingstoke: Macmillan, 1975)
WP	*Wessex Poems and Other Verses* (London: Harper & Brothers, 1898)
WW	*Winter Words in Various Moods and Metres* (London: Macmillan, 1928)

1

Introduction: Hardy our Contemporary?

In 1896 Thomas Hardy gave up novel-writing and began to relaunch his career as poet, which had been put on more or less indefinite hold back in the 1860s. By late 1895 Hardy's last-written novel, *Jude the Obscure,* had been published (*The Well-Beloved,* which appeared in book form in 1897, was first composed some years earlier), and it had caused a furore even greater than that which had greeted *Tess of the d'Urbervilles* four years previously. Wounded by what he saw as blinkered moralistic malice (and for other reasons which will be considered later), Hardy – who in many people's eyes, then and now, was at the height of his fictional powers – decided to quit. And over the last thirty-three years of his life, he produced eight volumes of poetry – totalling in excess of 960 poems – in addition to his huge verse-drama, *The Dynasts*. The first of these, *Wessex Poems*, appeared in 1898; the last, *Winter Words*, after his death in 1928. I rehearse these simple facts because they signal something of the nature and scale of the writer we have in hand, and of the difficulties which always traverse discussions of his work.

Born into a stonemason's family in Higher Bockhampton, Dorset, in 1840, Hardy died eighty-eight years later, the Grand Old Man of English letters. His birth was fourteen years before the Crimean War, and his earlier life was spent in the world of Palmerston, Disraeli, Gladstone, Garibaldi, and Bismarck, when Tennyson and Dickens were in their prime. His death came ten years after the end of the First World War, his later years lived out in the world of Ramsay MacDonald, Stalin, Hitler, and Mussolini, when T. S. Eliot, James Joyce, and Virginia Woolf were his literary contemporaries. The man whose early life coincides with the great period of railway expansion spent his old age being driven about in motor cars; the boy whose family played violins in the gallery 'quire' of a Dorset parish church grew into the old man who heard Big Ben ring in the New Year on his 'wireless'; born only six years after the Tolpuddle Martyrs were sentenced to transportation for forming a trade-union branch, Hardy was later to live through the General Strike of 1926. The novelist who recommended Thackeray's *Vanity Fair* to his sister in 1863, and whose novel *Far from the Madding Crowd* was first thought to have been by George Eliot, could now have recommended *Ulysses* and *To the Lighthouse* had he so desired; the poet whose career began first as Matthew Arnold's was ending and who lived within a stone's throw of Swinburne and Browning, was to receive a presentation copy of *Hugh Selwyn Mauberley* from Ezra Pound and have his sixth volume of poetry published in 1922, the same year as *The Waste Land*.

What all this indicates is, first, that Hardy was simply and pre-eminently *a writer*, one whose consistent and vast productivity over many decades gives the lie, if such is any longer needed, to the notion of a rural *naïf* speaking intimately from his native 'Wessex'. Secondly, it points to the fact that he had two careers – although, as we shall hear, he always regarded himself as primarily a poet. One, that of novelist, coincided almost exactly with the last four decades of the nineteenth century; the other, as poet, falls more or less exclusively in the first three of the twentieth century. Is Hardy, then, a Victorian novelist and a Modern poet? Or is it, by some odd paradox, the other way round: Victorian poet and Modern novelist? Is he principally a novelist or principally a poet? Criticism, even down to the present, when it poses questions about Hardy in such a way, can never make up its mind. Perhaps, therefore, they are unhelpful questions to ask.

An alternative way of historicizing Hardy – of trying to locate him historically – is to notice another significant fact about his work: that it is still very much with us at the beginning of the new millennium. There are many editions of Hardy's novels currently in print; there are numerous selections of his poems on sale, not to speak of the 'Complete' and 'Collected' volumes of the poetry; the Dorset Tourist Board has Hardy permanently at the centre of its publicity; he is read, taught, and studied at all levels throughout the English-speaking world, if nowhere else; and new critical books on every aspect of Hardy's work continue to appear in publishers' literature lists. Even more significantly, in the mid-1990s, the *Independent on Sunday* predicted that, following 'the year of [Jane] Austen (1995)', '1996 will be the year of the Wessex novelist and poet'.[1] There had already been a £3 million BBC2 adaptation of *The Return of the Native*, starring Catherine Zeta Jones, Clive Owen, and Joan Plowright, but as if to prove the paper's point, 1996 saw the release of Michael Winterbottom's BBC co-funded film of *Jude the Obscure*, with Christopher Ecclestone and Kate Winslet, and the opening of a new ballet of *Far from the Madding Crowd* in the Birmingham Royal Ballet's 'Midland Bank season'. There followed Phil Agland's £4 million production of *The Woodlanders* in 1997 (partly funded from the National Lottery by way of the Arts Council); and both an LWT TV adaptation of *Tess of the d'Urbervilles* and Nicholas Renton's Granada TV film of *Far from the Madding Crowd* in 1998 (other film versions have followed since). But it is worth noting – in the context of what is to follow in the present study – that, while the *Independent on Sunday* back in 1996 presented Hardy's novels authoritatively but predictably as about 'man's deepest passions, amid the countryside of Wessex, far from the fashionable concerns of the metropolis' (a sentence that could have been written at any point in the previous 100 years), it also quotes the film-makers as finding in Hardy's fiction 'essentially modern concerns' (young people thwarted by fate, 'powerful female characters', 'getting an education to better oneself'). As a sign, too, of Hardy's contemporaneity with the modern world, it is amusing to notice that the *Observer*, on the same Sunday in 1996, ran a full-page feature on the (by now legendary) story of the undertaker's cat which is supposed to have eaten Hardy's heart as it waited for burial in Stinsford churchyard, Dorset, in 1928 (his body was buried in Westminster Abbey). Pointedly, the paper ran the story in its 'News' section.[2]

The question all this poses is not whether Hardy is Victorian or Modern, but in what ways he is 'our contemporary': *what does he mean to us?* Depending who you are and where you are looking from, of course, the answer to these questions will vary dramatically. At one extreme will be the now traditional Hardy as poet and chronicler of a disappearing rural way of life, of Wessex, of the 'timeless' and 'universal' dramas of Character and Environment, of Love and Death, of Nature and Time, played out by rustic heroes and heroines – as at once the saviour of aspects of the English national heritage and himself a constituent of it. At the other extreme will be the radically subversive writer – or unwitting producer – of radically subversive texts which articulate for us difficult questions of class, gender, and sexuality in language and formal structures which are themselves profoundly unstable and destabilizing. 'Hardy', then, is terrain to be fought over, won, and occupied in the contemporary contestation of meaning and value. It will be the principal job of this study to explore what Thomas Hardy means to us early in the third millennium, and how and why he is made to do so.

2

The Life of Thomas Hardy

I have said already that Hardy is pre-eminently *a writer*, and this perhaps needs further elucidation. It is not just a matter of his having written so much over such a long period – although that is indeed an index of his professionalism; it is also a way of placing him socially, of remarking the impact of that positioning on his writing, and then of defining the kind of writer he is: what it is that constitutes his very *writerliness*. Let us consider these two linked points further.

Hardy may have belonged originally to that 'intermediate'[1] class in the rural economy of which he writes so sympathetically in his essay 'The Dorsetshire Labourer' (1883) and in *Tess of the d'Urbervilles*:

> an interesting and better-informed class ... including the carpenter, the smith, the shoemaker, the huckster, together with nondescript workers other than farm-labourers; a set of people who owed a certain stability of aim and conduct to the fact of their being life-holders like Tess's father, or copyholders, or, occasionally, small free-holders ... These families, who had formed the backbone of the village life in the past ... were the depositories of the village traditions. (*T.* 332–3)

But it would be quite wrong to see him as remaining in that class, or to see him, from the 1870s on, as basically still a countryman. Despite building a house, Max Gate, outside Dorchester in the early 1880s, and living there for the rest of his days, Hardy had spent formative periods in London in the 1860s and 1870s (as well as visiting it for several months of each spring and summer from Max Gate). His career, at least as a novelist, was made and shaped in the tough domain of the late-Victorian London literary market place, and he is better seen, in social terms, as a metropolitan man of letters than as a rural yeoman. Nevertheless, when literary success and financial reward allowed, he *did* build a house in Dorset and live there much of the time. The point surely is that Hardy, like so many other meritocratic cross-class writers and intellectuals, inhabited, in Raymond Williams's phrase, a kind of 'Border Country' – *déraciné, arriviste,* belonging neither to his class of origin nor to the social milieu in which his professional success had located him. It is this positioning in the interstices of a class society, I want to argue, that inscribes Hardy's novels at every point, and gives them the potential to be reread by contemporary readers as rather more than the fetichistically 'accurate' period dramas into which the television companies are currently attempting to turn all nineteenth-century fiction.

But first a word on Florence Emily Hardy's *The Life of Thomas Hardy, 1840–1928*, since this fascinatingly odd work will be referred to on many occasions, and is itself produced by and articulates what I will now call Hardy's 'border-country' mentality. Although presented as written by Hardy's second wife – it was first published after his death in two volumes, *The Early Life of Thomas Hardy, 1840–1891* (1928) and *The Later Years of Thomas Hardy, 1892–1928* (1930) – the biography was, in fact, composed by Hardy himself in the 1920s. He would go through his papers during the day, write some pages of the 'Life', have them typed in the evening by Florence Emily, and usually then destroy the original documents on which the narrative was based. The result, it was decided, would be passed off as the posthumous production of his widow. With this knowledge, therefore, the 'Prefatory Note' to *The Early Life* – over 'FEH's' initials – makes weird reading. It opens with the statement: 'Mr Hardy's feeling for a long time was that he would not care to have his life written at all. And though often asked to record his recollections he would say that he "had not sufficient admiration for himself to do so"' (*Life*, p. vii). Now it is one thing to have someone else quote you as saying this, and quite another to be quoting yourself, especially when you are writing your own biography! The Preface continues by noting that 'many erroneous and grotesque statements' about his experiences had forced his hand, and he had jotted down 'headings' and 'memories' for FEH to use 'in the event of its proving necessary to print them'. Of 'great help' were the 'dated observations which he made in pocket-books' when working as a novelist – such, of course, 'were not written with any view to their being printed' – and 'Mr Hardy's own reminiscent phrases have been used or approximated to whenever they could be remembered or were written down at the time of their expression *viva voce. On this point great trouble has been taken to secure exactness*' (*Life*, p. vii; emphasis added – Hardy had not really ceased to be a fiction writer!).

Anyone at all familiar with his writing style and characteristic turns of mind – especially in the prefaces to his novels and volumes of poems – will recognize them here, too, as indelibly Hardy's own. For example: 'the opinions quoted ... [are] passing thoughts only, temporarily jotted there for consideration, and not as permanent conclusions – a fact of which we are reminded by his frequent remarks on the tentative character of his theories' (*Life*, p. vii); or, 'incidents of his country experiences ... may be considered trivial ... but they have been included from a sense that they embody customs and manners of old West-of-England life that have now entirely passed away' (*Life*, p. viii). The fiction of this third-person biography is compounded at its end by the inclusion of some 'Notes by F.E.H.' after Hardy's death, which, by purporting to be different in kind from the papers from which the rest of the book had been compiled, seek to attest to the integrity of the authorship of the whole. And, throughout, very precise devices are deployed to sustain the illusion: from admissions of ignorance by 'the author' about things Hardy would clearly have known; through constant reminders that his notes were never intended for publication; to the wonderfully ironic reiteration (once one's in on the secret) of 'Hardy's frequent saying that he took little interest in himself as a person, and his absolute refusal at all times to write his reminiscences' (*Life*, 323) – this, by the man currently writing them for publication under his wife's name. Hardy's (auto)biography gives a wholly new dimension to the notion of the Official Life, and the scale and complexity of the deception are both striking and, I think, revealing.

Several significant points can be made by way of *The Life*. First, by page 35 of the one-volume edition (454 pages), Hardy's relatively lowly early origins in Dorset are completed and he is in London (many of these early pages point anyway to the 'noble' heritage of the Hardy family line in the past). The fact that one of his apparently more eccentric novels, *The Hand of Ethelberta* (1876), is a kind of displaced autobiography (the true 'Life') – in which a young woman of lower-class origin becomes a 'fictionist', breaks into high society by way of it, but has continually to suppress and conceal her real social background – perhaps adds a telling irony here. ('Hand', by the way, was Hardy's mother's maiden name, and Ethelberta, at the end of the novel, is engaged in writing an 'epic poem' – as Hardy was to do after he gave up fiction (see Chapter 5).) Secondly, despite Hardy's many disclaimers about his 'social ambition' and about 'the fashionable throng', much of *The Life* is filled with detailed and tedious accounts of the social events he later attended and with lists of names of the great and the good with whom he hobnobbed. Thirdly, a curious and revealing subtext of the work is Hardy's obsession with women and their sexuality. On the one hand, *The Life* says almost nothing about his two marriages – except, significantly, to give an account of the early, intensely romantic, courtship with Emma, his first wife, in Cornwall in the early 1870s (whose father, by the by, did not think Hardy 'good enough' to marry her). On the other, it continually records observation – a pointed word here, which I shall return to – of beautiful young women (including prostitutes) often only 'glimpsed' on trains, buses, and at social events: 'a Cleopatra in the railway carriage ... a good natured amative creature by her voice, and her heavy moist lips' (*Life*, 229); or, conversely and self-betrayingly, the 'handsome girl: cruel small mouth: she's of the class of interesting women one would be afraid to marry' (*Life*, 212). In particular, *The Life* notes – often disparagingly – the febrile beauty of the society ladies Hardy is now rubbing shoulders with: 'Mrs T. and her great eyes ... The most beautiful woman present ... But these women! If put into rough wrappers in a turnip-field, where would their beauty be?' (*Life*, 224). But, while mentioning in passing a number of stillborn early infatuations, it does *not* mention the relationship – whatever it was – with his cousin, Tryphena Sparks, the famous 'lost prize' of the poem 'Thoughts of Phena' (*WP*), nor those unrequited, arm's-length affairs with later 'lost prizes', the beautiful and aristocratic ladies, Mrs Florence Henniker and Lady Agnes Grove. Hardy's scopophilic fascination with (elusive) female sexuality and his own sexual timidity, it seems, may have been reinforced by the class exclusion he felt in respect of the 'ladies' he desires but who rejected him as a lover. All of which suggests a potent cocktail of prurient sexuality and class insecurity – in which matrix we may well find Hardy's *other* imaginative writings also conceived and formed. Fourthly, *The Life* is at pains to emphasize that Hardy was always 'really' a poet, and that he took up 'the trade of fiction' merely to establish himself financially. Indeed, perhaps the most perverse aspect of this everywhere perverse (auto)biography is its continually derogatory treatment of his novel-writing career. Despite thirty years of intensive labour at producing serious fiction, Hardy now emphasizes time and again that 'as he called his novel-writing "mere journeywork" he cared little about it as art' (*Life*, 179); claims 'indifference to a popular novelist's fame' (*Life*, 57); and says he gave it up for his first and true love: 'poetry and other forms of *pure* literature' (*Life*, 63; emphasis added) – a love 'instinctive and disinterested' (*Life*, 305). Having made it, then – having, in his own disparaging words, got 'to be considered a good hand at a serial' (*Life*, 100) – he now wishes to present himself, not as the toiling denizen of New Grub Street, but as the true *poet* – the aristocrat of literature.

The Life, in other words, presents Hardy as he now wanted to be seen: as the 'pure' literary man and classless equal of the best (especially female) society. It is, indeed, a striking fantasy of the socially and sexually insecure lower-class meritocrat, and every page ironically signals to it. But there is one final point to be made about it: the 'biography' is also evidence of the extreme self-consciousness of Hardy's writing, or, to put it another way, of writing which is the product of a self-consciousness so obsessive that it is often blind to its own disclosures. That is to say – to change the metaphor – that Hardy's controlling grip on his text is so white-knuckled that the latter is always likely to slip from his grasp and expose the very pressures, conflicts, and tensions it is designed to suppress. *The Life*, then, calls attention to the significance we should give in Hardy's writing both to his class insertion and linked sexual insecurity, and to his extreme writerliness – for, in effect, he literally *writes* his own life. Indeed, these comments may just as well be applied, as we shall see, to the highly wrought – perhaps overwrought – writing of all his texts.

3

Hardy amongst the Critics

Before turning to a consideration of the disturbed textuality of Hardy's novels and poems themselves, and of how they might meaningfully be read as contemporary discourses within our own culture, it is necessary to offer a brief survey of how he has been read and critically constituted hitherto. No writer's work – and certainly that of no writer who has held a significant place in literary history – can now be studied in and for itself: it is too determinately shaped by, and encrusted with, the critical and cultural reading practices, judgements, and evaluations already made about it, and which it carries with it like a palimpsest. In a real sense, such critical attention largely predetermines our perception of the canonic texts which come down to us; and, in the case of a writer like Hardy – who is also recruited to the service of a national culture and heritage – it is very difficult to see behind this kind of mythic construction of his 'characteristic' features.

Hardy's early success as a novelist came with *Under the Greenwood Tree* (1872), then even more emphatically with *Far from the Madding Crowd* (1874). It is easy to see here the critical lineaments of one potent mythic 'Hardy' establishing itself more or less from the start; annalist of rural ('peasant') life in the West Country; creator of 'Shakespearian' rustics; nostalgic chronicler of a passing rural order; writer of poetic description of the natural world; knowing inventor of sparky women characters; potentially 'gloomy' analyst of the tragedy of Love, Fate, and Nature mocking the aspirations and pretensions of human beings. 'Wessex' – that 'partly real, partly dream country' (*FMC*, Preface, '1895–1902'), comprising roughly the six counties of the Anglo-Saxon Heptarchy (Somerset, Devon, Hampshire, Berkshire, and

Wiltshire, with Dorset as its very centre) – does not explicitly arrive on (as) the scene until *The Return of the Native* (1878), for which Hardy supplied his own map of his fictional terrain. From here on, Hardy is ineluctably associated with Wessex, but, as his novel-writing career progressed with *The Mayor of Casterbridge* (1886), *The Woodlanders* (1887), *Tess* (1891), and *Jude* (1896), it is the darker side of his writing which is focused on and admired: his 'tragic' – almost 'Greek' – grasp of the 'universal' themes of human fallibility, Fate, Love, and Death. By the time he had stopped writing fiction, a very strong critical consensus along these lines obtained. Indeed, in 1912 – in the General Preface to the great Wessex Edition of all his works (this Preface is now regularly reprinted at the end of most paperback editions of Hardy's novels and in most modern selections of his poetry) – Hardy himself compounded this by retrospectively classifying his novels into three categories, the first and clearly most favoured of which was entitled 'Novels of Character and Environment'. This included *Tess, Jude, The Woodlanders, The Mayor of Casterbridge, The Return of the Native, Far from the Madding Crowd, Under the Greenwood Tree,* and three volumes of his short stories. He glosses them as 'those which approach most nearly to uninfluenced works' – that is, presumably, his most original and characteristic novels – and as ones which 'may claim a verisimilitude in general treatment and detail'. By the First World War, then, Hardy the Novelist was, in effect, 'the Novelist of Character and Environment': a poetic, tragic (and also pastorally comic) humanist-realist, whose core achievement, or canon, was represented incontrovertibly by five of the above seven novels (*Jude* has always been something of a maverick for critics; *Under the Greenwood Tree* sometimes a little lightweight).

The critical consensus about Hardy's fiction, however, also contained a negative dimension. There were two related aspects to this. First, there were seen to be characteristic 'flaws' in all his novels: a tendency to 'Sensationalism' and 'melodrama'; artificiality of plot – with too great a dependence on the creaking devices of 'chance' and contingency; 'flat' and unconvincing characterization; awkwardness and pedantry of style – or 'mannerism'; 'fashionable pessimism' or 'gloom'; and an obtrusive superfluity of 'ideas' or 'didacticism'. All of these are summed up by words and notions which occur with striking frequency in Hardy criticism before 1914 – if not right up to the present time (an introductory study in 1995, for example, refers to two of his late novels as of 'organic (if sometimes flawed) achievement'[1]): 'improbability', 'implausibility', lack of 'conviction', of 'credibility', of 'naturalness'. These are, of course, reflexes of a predilection for a seamless realism in fictional art, of the kind of 'verisimilitude' Hardy himself pointed to in his gloss on the 'Novels of Character and Environment' noted above; and the identification of his 'flaws' seeks at once to erase them from more substantive critical consideration and to lock his novels once and for all into the tradition of great realist fiction. I would like to emphasize this point here – to put in bold, as it were, the nature of Hardy's flaws and criticism's dismissive treatment of them – because my attempt below to reread his novels in the contemporary context will focus centrally on their pervasive presence throughout the texture of *all* his writing. Perhaps the flaws are themselves 'organic'?

The second negative dimension in the critical construction of Hardy the Novelist is the much grander excision from his 'true' canon of around half of the fourteen full-length fictions he produced. These are the ones he himself classified in the second and third categories of the 1912 General Preface mentioned above. *A Pair of Blue Eyes* (1873), *The Trumpet-Major* (1880), *Two on a Tower* (1882), *The Well-Beloved* (1897), and one volume of short stories fall into the second class – 'Romances and Fantasies' – which Hardy typically and tantalizingly glosses only as 'a sufficiently descriptive definition'. In the third category – 'Novels of Ingenuity' – are *Desperate Remedies* (1871), *The Hand of Ethelberta* (1876), and *A Laodicean* (1881), although in this case Hardy adds the telling and self-conscious comment (compare the critical vocabulary with my remarks on Hardy's 'flaws' above) that they 'show a not infrequent disregard of the probable in the chain of events ... They might also be characterized as "Experiments", and were written for the nonce simply; though despite the artificiality of their fable some of their scenes are not without fidelity to life.' 'Written for the nonce simply' implies that these were ephemeral potboilers, but we will have cause later to return to the notion of them as 'Experiments' and to reconsider whether Hardy's apparently harsh dismissal of them is, in fact, disingenuous. Be this as it may, there is no doubt that, during his lifetime and well down into this century, there was also a consensus that the 'minor' or 'lesser' novels were generally pretty awful, enacting all his flaws writ large and doing a great disservice to the 'characteristic' major novels of Wessex (with which several of the 'minor' ones suicidally had little to do). The seven novels listed above, therefore – with the possible exception of the pastoral historical Wessex romance *The Trumpet-Major*, and with others like *A Pair of Blue Eyes* and *The Well-Beloved* coming and going – were consigned to the critical outer darkness and were out of print for many years. Indeed, it is only since the 1970s, when Macmillan brought out the 'New Wessex' paperback edition of Hardy's works in anticipation of their going out of copyright in 1978, that all his novels have been available to the student and general reader; but I still find, even now, that non-expert Hardy lovers have often not heard of, let alone read, five or six of the 'lesser' novels.

Of all these 'uncharacteristic' inferior works, however, it is *The Hand of Ethelberta* and *A Laodicean* which reviewers and critics – with a few honourable exceptions – have most thoroughly execrated. In 1879 the former was seen as 'a fantastic interlude to his more serious work', while in 1889 J. M. Barrie attacked the latter (along with *Two on a Tower*) for being 'dull books: here and there, nasty as well, and the besom of oblivion will soon pass over them'.[2] In 1967, in a large standard literary history, the former is 'only a negligible piece of frivolity' and the latter 'quite worthless';[3] and even the introductions to the recuperative 'New Wessex' editions of the 1970s respectively state that the former is 'the joker in the pack' of Hardy's fiction, a 'comparative failure' and riddled with 'improbabilities' (*HE* 15, 18, 21, 27); while the latter is 'certainly not one of Hardy's great novels', has characters 'mechanically, if violently, contrived', a plot 'ludicrously implausible', and is full of 'improbable events', with the whole showing Hardy's 'carelessness of composition' (*L.* 13, 23, 30). More recently, some serious work has been devoted to the 'minor novels'; but for the most part Hardy the Novelist still remains that of the 'major' Wessex novels, with up to half of his *œuvre* omitted. The question this poses, and it is one I shall return to later in reassessing the 'Experiments' reviled above, is: what does it do to the *whole* Hardy canon if the 'improbable failures' are replaced cheek by jowl amongst the serious humanist-realist tragedies of rural Wessex? Do the 'flaws' in the latter, for example, become more obvious and importunate, more widespread and organic, more demanding of critical attention and explanation? Does Hardy's fiction, then, look more of a piece, and, if it does, what happens to the 'true' novelist of 'Character and Environment'? For the moment, let us remember one basic fact: these 'minor novels', with the exception of *Desperate Remedies*, are not Hardy's juvenilia, the results of his early apprenticeship to fiction-writing; they are spread throughout his career, even after he had discovered Wessex and its popularity with his readership. *Desperate Remedies* is, indeed, his first published novel (although not his first written one – for more on this, see Chapter 4); *A Pair of Blue Eyes* follows *Under the Greenwood Tree*; *The Hand of Ethelberta* succeeds Hardy's first major success in the Wessex mode, *Far from the Madding Crowd* (see Chapter 4 for his own comment on this); *A Laodicean* and *Two on a Tower* follow both the first explicitly Wessex tragedy, *The Return of the Native*, and his popular Wessex romance, *The Trumpet-Major*; *The Well-Beloved* follows *Tess* in periodical publication and *Jude* – Hardy's last novel – in its heavily revised book form. 'Romances', 'Fantasies', 'Novels of Ingenuity', 'Experiments', in other words, are interposed between most of those novels of 'verisimilitude', the 'Novels of Character and Environment': a realist extrapolation already perhaps looking increasingly artificial.

Without wishing to construct an oversimplified critical strawman as target, it is reasonably fair to say that the characteristic achievements of Hardy the Novelist which we have already encountered are continually reconfirmed in criticism from the First World War onwards. Certainly, Lord David Cecil's famous and influential book, unsurprisingly titled *Hardy the Novelist* (1943 – but still regularly cited in the brief Further Reading sections of student 'Study Guides'), reproduces almost exactly that familiar *persona*:

> We are shown life in its fundamental elements, as exemplified by simple, elemental characters actuated by simple, elemental passions... And the fact that they are seen in relation to ultimate Destiny gives them a gigantic and universal character. Nor is the universality of this picture weakened by the fact that Hardy writes only of country people in nineteenth-century Wessex. On the contrary... concentrated in this

> narrow, sequestered form of life, basic facts of the human drama showed up at their strongest.[4]

Douglas Brown's equally influential study, *Thomas Hardy* (1954), also reinforces earlier notions of him as chronicler of the decline of a sturdy and robust rural community in the face of urban culture, and mobilizes Hardy's Wessex in opposition to 'modern life': 'this pattern records Hardy's dismay at the ... precarious hold of the agricultural way of life. It records ... a deep-seated allegiance of the writer's personality, a degree of dependence upon an identified and reliable past.'[5] Such traits remain with us in conventional representations of Hardy right down to the present. We may recall the *Independent on Sunday* critic's pure Cecil: 'man's deepest passions, amid the countryside of Wessex, far from the fashionable concerns of the metropolis'; or note this Brownian advertisement for a 1980s university adult education course:

> Today our lives are so rushed and hectic and noisy. It is refreshing to escape into the old, traditional, rural world with the peace and calm that Hardy depicts so beautifully in his novels. His love of nature and folk-lore recreate an almost timeless world which unfortunately, even as he wrote, he saw fast disappearing.[6]

The concept of a 'timeless world...fast disappearing' is an interesting one.

In the 1960s and 1970s, however, different inflexions were added: while F. R. Leavis had earlier famously omitted Hardy from 'the great tradition' as 'a provincial manufacturer of gauche and heavy fictions',[7] other younger critics now began to examine the formal complexities of his fiction. Amongst other works by such, Jean Brooks's *Thomas Hardy: The Poetic Structure* (1971), Ian Gregor's *The Great Web: The Form of Hardy's Major Fiction* (1974 – note the subtitle), Penelope Vigar's *The Novels of Thomas Hardy: Illusion and Reality* (1974), and Peter Casagrande's *Unity in Hardy's Novels: 'Repetitive Symmetries'* (1982) deploy a kind of high-powered humanist formalism which ousts the older 'character'/'environment'/'Fate'/'Tragedy'/'rural-elegy' nexus in favour of 'poetic structure', 'unity', 'symbolism', 'imagery', and 'pattern'. In effect, however, and at a fundamental level, such 'new' criticism reveals similar underlying assumptions about Hardy's fiction: about its humanism ('unity' and 'poetic structure' are seen to articulate this world-view); about its 'flaws'; about its uneasy relation to realism; and about its focus and themes. Casagrande, for example, writes that Hardy's 'world and its people are intensely English, intensely West Country, and uniquely his at the same time they are universal' (*sic*) and that they 'reflect a nostalgic sensibility and a traditional upbringing violated by "change and chancefulness"'.[8] Furthermore, the pursuit of patterns of formal structures and motifs tended to establish the homogeneity of Hardy's writing, to smooth and refine his work, rather than recognizing its fractured and dissonant discourses, its potentially *anti*-realist thrust. It is not surprising, therefore, that the so-called 'minor novels' received either scant and unsympathetic attention in this criticism, or, more usually, none at all.

As part of the fallout from newer Marxist, feminist, and poststructuralist theoretical work, criticism of Hardy's fiction has, in the 1980s and 1990s, taken on a rather more radical and subversive guise. Social and sociological readings – strikingly absent hitherto, except principally in the pioneering studies by Merryn and Raymond Williams (see Select Bibliography) – now proliferate: Hardy and social class; Hardy and the rural economy; Hardy and the Dorsetshire labourer; Hardy and politics – radical scourge of agricultural and property-owning exploitation or bourgeois apologist for an always pastoralized rurality? Feminist criticism, in particular, has fundamentally recast the study of Hardy's fiction – obviously and especially in his treatment of women, and of sex and sexuality more generally. Hardy had always been renowned for his ability to create vivacious, unconventional, and erotically charged female characters, and for his radical flouting of Victorian Grundyism in his treatment of sex (Tess 'a pure woman'? – shock, horror!), but these critical stereotypes were themselves now challenged and displaced. The issues instead became: Is Hardy a feminist *avant le lettre*? How could a late-Victorian male articulate an enlightened feminism? Is he guilty of misogyny like so many others of his male contemporaries? Are his female protagonists victims of patriarchy or 'New Women'? Why does he create dynamic heroines like Paula Power, Bathsheba Everdene, or Tess only to marry or kill them off? Does he expose social injustice to women, or is he complicit in it by never letting his free spirits succeed? How does he render and depict female sexuality? Is it always as a reflex of the Male Gaze – that of his male characters or of Hardy's own scopophilic eye? How is the textual discourse itself eroticized? Many of these questions, of course, also inform the social approaches mentioned above, so that issues around class, gender, and their interrelationship currently lie at the heart of Hardy criticism. Such work is exemplified by that of, amongst others, Kathleen Blake, Penny Boumelha, Terry Eagleton, Joe Fisher, Marjorie Garson, John Goode, Margaret Higgonet, Patricia Ingham, Mary Jacobus, Patricia Stubbs, and George Wotton (all to be found in the Select Bibliography). Two further points may be made about this newer criticism. First, by way of the postmodernist and deconstructive propellants in the subversive rereadings deployed, the focus is placed on the unstable play of the language in Hardy's fictional texts as their central feature. His complex, riven, and heteroglossic textuality, in other words, becomes the object of critical attention and is itself seen as the 'subject' of the novels. Secondly – and paradoxically – despite all this, the 'lesser novels', where so much of Hardy's fictional practice and cast of mind is almost self-parodically delineated, still receive only minimal treatment.[9] Even a radicalized Hardy remains the canonic one.

The critical reception of Hardy's poetry, and its subsequent lineage in twentieth-century criticism, differ in significant ways from those of his fiction – although, as we shall see, they also have some strong resemblances and effects. For a start, in 1898, when *Wessex Poems* first appeared, Hardy was already a famous novelist who had just given up writing novels, and the reviewers' responses to his shift of genre were mixed. As he himself sardonically observed, while some critics were friendly, showing respect and praise, others were 'not without umbrage at [his] having taken the liberty to adopt another vehicle of expression than prose-fiction without consulting them' (*Life*, 299). Still others attacked it fiercely: the *Saturday Review* infamously commented on 'this curious and wearisome volume, these many slovenly, slipshod, uncouth verses, stilted in sentiment, poorly conceived and worse wrought'; rejected some of Hardy's ballads as 'the most amazing balderdash that ever found its way into a book of verse'; and wondered why 'the bulk of the volume was published at all – why he did not himself burn the verse'. E. K. Chambers also noted that Hardy's 'success in poetry is of a very narrow range', and – first voicing a view that was to become a central issue in the critical history and evaluation of Hardy as a poet and which I discuss more fully below – limited this 'success' to a 'small cluster of really remarkable poems'. Of *Poems of the Past and the Present* in 1901, the *Academy* judged: 'there is more of sheer poetry in his novels', while the *Athenaeum* thought Hardy 'is wholly mistaking his vocation' in switching from fiction to verse.[10] However, the volumes of poetry continued to roll out: *Time's Laughingstocks and Other Verses* in 1909 – Hardy having completed the monumental labour of writing his epic verse-drama, *The Dynasts*, between 1902 and 1907; *Satires of Circumstances, Lyrics and Reveries* (1914); *Moments of Vision and Miscellaneous Verses* (1917); *Late Lyrics and Earlier* (1922); *Human Shows, Far Phantasies, Songs and Trifles* (1925); and *Winter Words in Various Moods and Metres* (posthumously, in 1928). In 1916 Hardy published what is, in effect, the first anthology of his poetry, *Selected Poems*, which he enlarged and rearranged in 1927 as *Chosen Poems* (published posthumously in 1929); and in 1919 the first edition of his *Collected Poems* appeared, which was again revised and enlarged for the editions of 1923, 1928, and 1930. As the volume of poetry mounted, and readers began to regard him as poet rather than novelist, Hardy's popularity grew. Individual poems were increasingly first published in daily newspapers and other popular journals: such well-known ones as 'In Time of "The Breaking of Nations"' and 'The Oxen', for example, first appeared respectively in the *Saturday Review* and *The Times* as contributions to the war effort without copyright restriction to encourage wide and free reprinting. Equally, sales of the volumes themselves soared, and Hardy the Poet became something of a best-seller (for example, the Macmillan 'Pocket Edition' of *Wessex Poems* and *Poems of the Past and the Present* was reprinted four times between 1907 and 1918, and *Moments of Vision* went to a second impression within a month of publication).

Critically, too, Hardy's poetic achievement was widely recognized, albeit with strong elements of typical paradox present. A contemporary of the 'Georgian Poets' – that loose grouping of younger poets anthologized by Edward Marsh in the *Georgian Poetry* volumes from 1912 on – Hardy has often been seen, then and now, as their *éminence grise*, as a kind of elder, senior Georgian (indeed, he continued to publish poems regularly in J. C. Squire's *London Mercury* in the 1920s – a journal which promoted a Georgianism looking decidedly *passé* after Imagism, war poetry, and the onset of full-blown modernist poetry). At the same time, however, Ezra Pound, the arch-Imagist and modernist, was famously celebrating Hardy as a contemporary poet, later noting that such poetry as his could only be 'the harvest of having written twenty [*sic*] novels first'.[11] Furthermore, F. R. Leavis, in *New Bearings in English Poetry* (1932), that seminal beginner's manual on how to read modern poetry (i.e. *The Waste Land*), had singled out Hardy as the principal poetic voice of the older generation. Nevertheless, with sure Leavisian even-handedness, he also notes that the 'vast bulk of verse [is] interesting only by its oddity and idiosyncrasy', and that Hardy's 'rank as a major poet rests upon a dozen ["great"] poems' (characteristically, Leavis does not say which they are).[12] Herein is identified the absolute nub of criticism's difficulties with Hardy's poetry – repeated, as we shall see, with astonishing and formulaic frequency by critics and editors ever since. Indeed, much of my treatment both of the criticism and of Hardy's poetry will centre on the perceived problems of dealing with his huge *œuvre*, and of at once identifying *which* poems constitute the core of his achievement and what the nature of his 'greatness' might be. If the reader hears an echo in all this of the 'flaws' beloved of Hardy novel criticism, and of the selective discrimination of 'major' from 'minor' novels to construct a canon of his truly 'characteristic' fictional achievement, then all to the good: for it is, indeed, a common feature of both sets of criticism and leads to similar effects on, and constructions of, 'Thomas Hardy'.

However, before tracing the features of the poetry criticism, it is worth indicating what Hardy's 'faults' as poet are perceived to be, and to note in passing their consanguinity with the flaws in his fiction. On the whole, of course, critics do not deal substantively with the faults; rather, they are mentioned in dismissive value judgements which assume a given unanimity of taste in the discrimination of what is 'good' and 'bad' in poetry. From early on – and these are often repeated even in the introductions to contemporary Selections of his poems – the characteristics of Hardy's 'bad' poetry are as follows: oddity, idiosyncrasy, gaucherie, the tendency to write too much, awkwardness, conventionality, pedantry, a mixture of the poetical and the colloquial, rusticity, melodrama, 'gloomy' over-deterministic philosophy, stiffness, and eccentricity (of subject and language). The fact that more positive representations of the *same* characteristics are usually held to comprise his central virtues indicates how slippery the path to the 'true' greatness of Hardy the Poet may be. As Mark Van Doren tellingly admitted: 'too many of Hardy's poems . . . are not "good" . . . but I am always changing my mind as to which ones those are.'[13] As with the fiction, the 'faults' which mar the 'bad' poems are perceptible in the 'good' ones, too.

In his widely influential book *Thomas Hardy and British Poetry* (1973), while attempting to mark out a counter-tradition in modern poetry to that of Anglo-American modernism, Donald Davie notes a central difficulty in identifying Hardy's 'greatness' and particularly in agreeing on those poems which represent the quintessential core of his achievement: precisely *which* poems comprise the 'true' Hardy? Critic after critic, Davie observes, 'complains that nearly 1000 poems are too much, and asks for a more or less agreed-upon select few, a canon on which Hardy's reputation shall rest'. But the problem is that no one *can* agree. Further, the fact that one selection of Hardy, while being neither 'perfunctory' nor 'eccentric', leaves out several of the 'greatest' of the 'Poems of 1912–13', leads Davie to the central conclusion that, 'cast about as one may . . . one perceives no consensus emerging as to what is centrally significant in Hardy's poetry, still less therefore as to what is the canon of his secure achievements'. Unable to discriminate the good from the bad – because of the large number of poems and our inability to date them as early or late or to categorize them securely by genre – 'each reader finds in the poems what he brings to them; what he finds there is his own pattern of preoccupations and preferences. If this is true of every poet to some degree, of Hardy it is exceptionally true.'[14]

Davie is at once exactly right about the critical problematic of defining what is centrally significant in Hardy's poetry, and – at least by now – rather off the mark about 'the canon of his secure achievements'. I wish briefly to show that, by now (if not in Davie's 1973), there is indeed a core of 'centrally significant' poems, a Hardy poetic 'canon', which has been created – largely tacitly and cumulatively – by editors and critics, a 'true' Hardy represented by poems which Samuel Hynes has symptomatically called 'characteristically Hardyesque',[15] which then closes out the large ruck of his so-called inferior work. The difficulty of identifying 'the essential Hardy' has persisted most apparently in the labours of editors of Selections of his poetry right up to the present moment; and Selections, while they may look natural, almost self-selecting, objective, scholarly, neutral, and disinterested, in the nature of things are nothing of the kind. They involve personal choice, contemporary cultural presuppositions, and more or less (usually less) random sampling of a writer's work; and they effectively *construct* a writer rather more substantively – but also, because of their usually unspoken informing assumptions, more subliminally – than most other critical attention does. What we take to be the 'primary text' has, in fact, already been heavily shaped and processed by the editors' and publishers' literary predilections and market intentions.

It is illuminating to consider the problems perceived by the editors of several widely available, more or less contemporary, anthologies and the principles of selection and organization on which the poems they include are based. Harry Thomas, for example, in the Penguin Classics *Selected Poems* (1993), notes William Empson, more than fifty years before, remarking that 'a working selection, from Hardy's mass of bad poetry is much needed', and offers his own, therefore, as just such a 'working selection' of 'the best poems'.[16] David Wright, in a second Penguin edition, *Selected Poems* (1978), also states that, while 'there is no doubt that [he] is one of the major poets of the twentieth century...it is only difficult to make up one's mind how good, and/or how bad, almost any particular poem of Hardy's is'; and, in his 'Note on the Selection', neatly sums up the 'difficulty' of his task as 'not least because one man's Hardy is often as not another man's bathos'.[17] T. R. M. Creighton, in his *Poems of Thomas Hardy: A New Selection* (1974), organizes it in such a way as to allow Hardy's 'art to reveal itself by reducing its bulk and defining its main kinds and preoccupations... not to present "the best of Hardy" but a cross-section of all he wrote in reduced compass and systematic arrangement'. The vast bulk of the *Collected Poems*, Creighton argues, 'obscure[s] its greatness'; what he does, therefore, is to rearrange the poems in categories which 'reveal' Hardy's themes. But it is here that the critical engineering shows most clearly, largely because of the presuppositions on which the editor announces his volume to be based:

> My broad classifications – Nature, Love, Memory and Reflection, Dramatic and Personative, and Narrative – can claim almost canonical authority. I have allowed the poems to arrange themselves and have remained as passive under their guidance as I could. They seemed to require to begin with the universal themes of nature and love...[18]

There can surely be no clearer example than this of an editor passing off as 'natural' his own critical and ideological interpretative shaping of a writer's work.

Even in those volumes which employ the most straightforward principle of organizing the poems – in the order of Hardy's own published volumes – their actual selection remains problematical; and, as evidence of how a canon 'naturally' forms itself, the majority contain absolutely no explanation of the principles on which the selection has been made. For example, Richard Willmott's *Selected Poems* (1992), in the Oxford Student Texts series, offers no indication as to why the novice Hardy reader (presumably its target market is principally schools) should be reading these particular poems – nor, indeed, that the fifty-four included have been selected in the first place from more than 900 others. It is a very clear case of the way 'primary texts' in secondary and tertiary education, if nowhere else, 'edit' their readers. Much the same is true of the high-profile anthologies edited by Andrew Motion (the new Everyman) and the two by Samuel Hynes for Oxford, which must currently be, together with the Penguin selections by Thomas and Wright, the five volumes most likely to be bought by students and general public alike. In the introduction to *Selected Poems* (1994), Motion once more registers the 'alarm' with which even Hardy's 'most enthusiastic admirers still respond to the enormous bulk' of his *Collected Poems* and the perceived impossibility of making an 'adequate selection... when no one agreed which were his best poems';[19] but there is no explanation of how *his* selection (of roughly a quarter of Hardy's *œuvre*) was arrived at or of how, finally, he identified the 'best poems'. Samuel Hynes (editor of the invaluable Oxford University Press edition of *The Complete Poetical Works of Thomas Hardy*) has further edited (the Monopolies Commission take note) two paperback selections of Hardy's poems, also for Oxford: *A Critical Selection of his Finest Poetry* (1984) in The Oxford Author's series, and *A Selection of his Finest Poems* (1994) in the Oxford Poetry Library series; both books are in print and both covers reproduce a version of the same portrait of Hardy. Equally, both volumes are entirely silent on the principles of selection used, whilst delivering such question-begging and monumentally self-assured value judgements as: 'they are not very good poems, and... are not... characteristically Hardyesque' (these are the ones that 'do not speak with Hardy's unique poetic voice'); others 'are surely "universal", if any poems are'.[20] This unexamined – and certainly not '*Critical*' – identification of Hardy's '*finest*' poems is all the more worrying if we note that the second of the two volumes contains only just over half of the poems in the earlier one; that both are nevertheless entitled Hardy's 'Finest'; and that the poems omitted from the later volume are, by and large, the less familiar ones also omitted from most other selections. Something, surely, was needed to explain how the 'Finest' are to be extrapolated from the 'Finest'. But the myopic (and market-driven) self-certainty of what is going on here is also compounded by the crude fact that the 1984 introduction is reproduced *verbatim* as the introduction to the 1994 volume (and given a new 1994 copyright date). 'Finest' is as 'Finest' does; but surely the 1994 volume should have been called 'The Finest of Hardy's Finest Poems'?

Despite all the 'difficulty' and disagreement as to which are Hardy's 'best', most 'characteristic', and 'greatest' poems, there is, by now, a sizeable group which, by a tacit process of accretion, seems to represent that 'canon of secure achievements' which Davie in 1973 looked for in vain. This has not been an explicit critical consensus, arrived at by persuasive and convincing analysis, but one contrived by the repeated appearance of those poems in anthologies and selections,[21] so that they do now seem to 'select themselves' by natural right rather than having to be argued for on their merits. This means that they carry at once a great deal of evaluative critical baggage – many assumptions about Hardy, literature, criticism, and literary studies are subliminally inscribed in them – and that these poems tend to exclude, or rank in inferior order, well over three-quarters of Hardy's work. Later, I will consider in more detail the implications of this editorial construction of Hardy the Poet, what his characteristics are, and what it is that has made Poem A one of the 'finest', and Poem B decidedly not. Suffice to say, here, that any explanation will combine both mundane empirical reasons (e.g. the continuing reproduction of many of the most familiar poems Hardy himself first selected for his own edited anthology, *Chosen Poems*), and cultural/ideological ones: Hardy as the poet of Wessex, Nature, Time, Love, and Death, representing ironic quietism and rural nostalgia as an antidote to the modern 'Dark Age' of twentieth-century madness and alienation – a not unrecognizable sibling of certain versions of Hardy the Novelist.

To conclude this partial survey of Hardy criticism: what *does* distinguish the Poet from the Novelist is the paucity of contemporary criticism on the former, which is driven by the newer theoretical approaches briefly surveyed in relation to the fiction. Many of the critical monographs and essays on Hardy's poetry display painstaking exegesis, interpretation, and appreciation of his themes and prosody – strongly reminiscent of the humanist–formalist approaches of novel criticism in the 1960s and 1970s. Tom Paulin's highly regarded book *Thomas Hardy: The Poetry of Perception* (1975) is just such a linear critical narrative of the themes, motifs, and tropes in a wide range of the poems; Dennis Taylor's immensely learned two books, *Hardy's Poetry 1860–1928* (1981) and *Hardy's Metres and Victorian Prosody* (1988), recognize that theoretical initiatives are all around, but continue to offer a largely descriptive and exegetical analysis of the poetry; and Trevor Johnson's *A Critical Introduction to the Poems of Thomas Hardy* (1991), in its devoted reaffirmation in tone and judgement of most of the conventional features of Hardy the Poet, could have been written thirty years before. Notable exceptions, then, are critics, assisted by contemporary approaches, who seek to read Hardy against the familiar graining:

for example, J. Hillis Miller in *The Linguistic Moment* (1985) and *Tropes, Parables, Performatives: Essays on Twentieth-Century Literature* (1990); Tim Armstrong, whose introduction to his *Thomas Hardy: Selected Poems* (1993) offers an excellent synoptic exposition of the various filaments in modern criticism of Hardy's poetry; and John Lucas in *Modern English Poetry from Hardy to Hughes* (1986). There is also a significantly lone essay in Margaret Higgonet's collection, *The Sense of Sex: Feminist Perspectives on Hardy* (1993), albeit by a male critic whose project, with some Freudian scaffolding, is to suggest that 'the propelling force behind [Hardy's] finest lyrics' is 'the recovery of the feminine', an attempt to 'work out a gender opposition he would like to abolish . . . to annul sexual difference'[22] (what renders this problematical is the simple intentionalism which presents Hardy as entirely in charge of this 'feminist' discourse). In the context of such a dearth of regenerative rereading of Hardy's poetry, then, one awaits with keen anticipation a forthcoming book about it by the New Historicist critic, Marjorie Levinson. One also awaits a criticism which ceases to focus almost exclusively on the canonic poems and engages with that 'mass of bad poetry' – equivalent to the disregarded 'minor novels' – in terms other than those of pre-emptive and judgemental downgrading. As Mark Van Doren once perceptively noted: 'there is no core of pieces, no inner set of classic or perfect poems, which would prove his rank. . . . It is the whole of him that registers and counts';[23] we might add, 'flaws' and all.

4

Hardy the Novelist

Famously, Hardy's 'lost' first-written novel was never published and the manuscript at some point destroyed. It was to have been entitled *The Poor Man and the Lady* 'By the Poor Man' – and the only discrete remnant of it that has survived is the (reworked) long short story, 'An Indiscretion in the Life of an Heiress'. How, then, do we know anything about it? The answer is that in the 1920s, in his eighties and approaching the end of a long and now internationally renowned career as novelist and poet, Hardy devoted several sympathetic pages to it in what we have seen earlier to be his last 'fiction', *The Life of Thomas Hardy.*[1] As always with *The Life*, we should treat what it tells us with care; but what we are left with, nevertheless, is an account, composed towards the end of Hardy's life, of a (seemingly favoured) 'first' novel which thus positions itself as a kind of self-reflexive gloss on all Hardy's published fiction after *The Poor Man*. The comments on it in *The Life*, then, repay close attention.

It first refers to the work as 'a striking socialistic novel', adding 'not that he mentally defined it as such, for the word had probably never, or scarcely ever, been heard of at that date' (*Life*, 56); but we should register that that is precisely how Hardy *did* 'mentally define' it in the 1920s. *The Life* then reproduces generous praise for aspects of the novel by the publisher, Alexander Macmillan, who first read the manuscript, and similar comment by another reader, John Morley, who nevertheless noted – perceptively perhaps, given Hardy's obsession with social status – that the 'wildly extravagant' scenes in it 'read like some clever lad's dream' (*Life*, 59). George Meredith then looked at the manuscript for Chapman & Hall – Hardy was fortunate with his early readers – and the account of their meeting contains the most illuminating description of that first lost novel:

> The story was ... a sweeping dramatic satire of the squirearchy and nobility, London society, the vulgarity of the middle-class, modern Christianity, church-restoration, and political and domestic morals in general, the author's views, in fact, being obviously those of a young man with a passion for reforming the world ... the tendency of the writing being socialistic, not to say revolutionary; yet not argumentatively so, the style having the affected simplicity of Defoe's (which had long attracted Hardy ... to imitation of it) ...
>
> The satire was obviously pushed too far – as sometimes in Swift and Defoe themselves ... (*Life*, 61)

The Life adds – significantly, in the context of a reputation built on the Wessex novels – that 'the most important scenes were laid in London', which Hardy knew 'like a born Londoner': 'an experience quite ignored by the reviewers of his later books, who, if he only touched on London in his pages, promptly reminded him not to write of a place he was unacquainted with, but to get back to his sheepfolds' (*Life*, 62).

Meredith warned Hardy 'not to "nail his colours to the mast" so definitely in a first book, if he wished to do anything practical in literature; for if he printed so pronounced a thing he would be attacked on all sides by the conventional reviewers, and his future injured' – *The Life* adding the pointed observation that, though such a novel might be accepted 'calmly' in the 1920s, 'in genteel mid-Victorian 1869 it would no doubt have incurred ... - severe strictures which might have handicapped a young writer for a long time' (*Life*, 62). On Meredith's advice, therefore, Hardy put *The Poor Man and the Lady* to one side and set about constructing 'the eminently "sensational" plot' (*Life*, 63) which was to become *Desperate Remedies*. Nevertheless, the old Hardy pauses to reflect that three such eminent Victorian men of letters should have seen so much to admire in the work of an 'unknown young man', and that 'such experienced critics' had found it 'aggressive and even dangerous ... (Mr Macmillan had said it "meant mischief")' (*Life*, 62). Later, writing about the reception of *The Hand of Ethelberta* – 'a Comedy of Society' 'thirty years too soon' for its period – he observes the same of *The Poor Man*: 'it had been too soon for a socialist story.' Implicit in this, surely, is Hardy's continuing approbation of it – carefully saying, not that it was 'bad', but that it was ahead of its time: 'too soon for [its] date' (*Life*, 108).

So what happened to the young 'socialistic' novelist? Well, as we have heard above, he had to get 'to be considered a good hand at a serial'; the tyro novelist had to make his way in the rough world of Victorian Grub Street, and so, in some senses, he had to conform. Furthermore, as he got older and more successful, he enjoyed his lionization by High Society, and, as *The Life* makes clear on a number of occasions, saw himself as entirely apolitical – a stance at once typical of, and advantageous to, an insecure meritocrat and *arriviste*. But there is also a sense, I would like to argue, in which that radical young fiction-writer goes underground. He finds an 'acceptable' novelist's guise – the humanist–realist tragedian of Wessex – and then, from within it, both self-subverts his own fiction and destabilizes the wider cultural-ideological positions which make it acceptable in the first place. Hence all those 'flaws' and those disconcerting 'minor novels'. I am suggesting, then, that there is indeed a kind of duplicity even in the Wessex novels, which latter throw up a screen of signifiers, as it were, thus encouraging the kinds of conservative readings I have described in Chapter 3 and disguising the other textual strategies going on behind it. This is very much what Joe Fisher argues – perhaps over-ingeniously – in his book *The Hidden Hardy* (1992). His general working notion is of a distinction in Hardy's works between his 'traded' texts, 'sold on' to the bourgeois fiction market – in which Wessex is the principal commodity and the 'Novels of Character and Environment' the most obvious cases – and his 'narrated' texts – that is, the 'Novels of Ingenuity' with their subversive narrative strategies. Fisher sees the 'major' novels as representing 'an inherently conflictual engagement of the two', in which the proficient market 'trader' exploits a gap between the man who sells and the narrator who tells, thus simultaneously making the 'traded object' acceptable and 'corrupting' it. The 'Hidden Hardy', then, is a 'self-subversion . . . a sustained campaign of deception which runs through all [the] novels, creating hostile and part-visible patterns beneath what might generally be regarded as the "surface" of the text'. The problem with this otherwise convincing reading is that it is too instrumentalist, leaving Hardy somehow too unequivocally *in charge* of the complex self-subversion of his novels.[2] How far this guerrilla positioning – if so it be – is conscious and intentional on Hardy's part, therefore, remains a moot point and one incapable of conclusive resolution. Let us just work on the principle that an answer lies somewhere between the presence of extensive circumstantial textual evidence that Hardy was extremely self-conscious and self-reflexive in everything he wrote, and a recognition that our contemporary critical optics will 'see' a writer's work in such a way as to bring into view discourses which would not be discerned otherwise.

But, for the moment, let us assess what can be taken from Hardy's comments on *The Poor Man and the Lady*. First, fairly obviously, there is his class animus – the repeated use of the word 'socialistic' implying, I believe, not so much a defined political position as a radical, subversive stance, especially towards the classes 'above' him: the 'squirearchy and nobility, London society, the vulgarity of the middle class'. Only two pages earlier, *The Life* reproduces one of Hardy's 'Notes of 1866–7', which suggests his already highly nuanced fascination with class relations: 'The defects of a class are more perceptible to the class immediately below it than to itself' (*Life*, 55). Alexander Macmillan criticized the 'class bias' of the novel, and the proposed title – with its pointed use of 'the Lady', plus describing itself as 'By the Poor Man' – at once indicates its subject and points forward to all those other cross-class sexual relationships at the heart of Hardy's fiction. Secondly, we may consider that the novel which most recognizably reworks this 'socialistic' lost one, even though in a complex and inverted fashion, is *The Hand of Ethelberta* – Hardy's own fictionalized 'Life'; and it is significant, too, that his *last* novel, *Jude the Obscure*, with its 'socialistic' hero, is probably as close in cast of mind to this first one as any of the others intervening. Hardy always strenuously denied – not very convincingly – that *Jude*, too, was autobiographical (see *Life*, 252, 274, 392). Thirdly, there is Hardy's notably irritable sensitivity to the reviewers' dismissal of anything he wrote which was not about 'sheepfolds , and his implicit claim that he is as much a metropolitan as he is a countryman. Perhaps those Wessex 'Novels of Character and Environment' were not so privileged by Hardy as it would seem – he had, after all, cynically commented to Sir Frederick Macmillan in April 1912 that 'the advantage of classifying the novels seems to be that it affords the journalists something to discuss'.[3] Fourthly, we may register Hardy's emphatic self-consciousness about the style of the book, and especially the explicit invocation of Defoe – the phrase 'affected simplicity' surely being a key to Hardy's own sharp sense of the artifice/artificiality of fictional discourse, and especially that claiming to be authentic 'realism'. In two highly self-reflexive passages in that most artificial of fictions, *The Hand of Ethelberta*, the heroine also invokes Defoe while defining herself as a 'professed romancer', and is later described as modelling herself on 'that master of feigning' (Defoe), whose 'talent... for telling lies' shapes her own ability to make the entirely fictive have 'the one pre-eminent merit of seeming like truth' (*HE*, chs. 13, 16). Furthermore, in 1919 (note that he had stopped writing novels over twenty years previously), the 79-year-old Hardy is presented in *The Life* thus:

> A curious question arose in Hardy's mind at this date on whether a *romancer* was morally justified in going to extreme lengths of assurance – after the manner of Defoe – in respect of a tale he knew to be *absolutely false*.... Had he not long discontinued the writing of romances he would, he said, have put at the beginning of each new one: 'Understand that however true this book may be in essence, in fact it is *utterly untrue*.' (*Life*, 391–2; emphases added)

Hardy's self-consciousness about the art of faking, and his confessed consanguinity with the master illusionist Defoe, cannot be in question. It is also arguable that he *did*, in effect, draw the reader's attention to the fictionality of his fictions – in part in his slyly ironic prefaces to them, but rather more 'organically' in the highly self-reflexive parading, to a greater or lesser extent in all his novels, of the artifice which comprises them. The radical 'underground' Hardy, I would argue, can be read as simultaneously creating illusion and deconstructing it – which makes his novels appear so awkward and uncomfortable to read. Perhaps the 'certain rawness of absurdity' and the 'very excess' of the satire which Macmillan and Morley[4] found in Hardy's 'first' novel were not a beginner's blemishes but a constant and crucial constituent of *all* his fiction: the bedrock of its formal signification.

My fifth and final expropriation from Hardy's comments on *The Poor Man* is a central one for the rest of my argument on his novels: Hardy twice uses the word 'satire' to describe the work.

Presumably, in this particular case, he meant the conventional sense of a *social* satire which reveals and excoriates the 'degeneracy of the age' (*Life*, 62) by way of exaggeration and irony. But in Hardy's work more generally, the notion of satire takes on a wider and more resonant significance: we may think, more or less at random, of an improbable coincidence in *A Laodicean* described as giving 'an added point to the satire' (*L.* 255); of Egdon Heath, at the beginning of *The Return of the Native*, as laying 'a certain vein of satire on human vanity in clothes' (*RN* 33); of the title of the volume of poems, *Satires of Circumstance* (1914). In none of these cases is the word used in the sense of the literary genre defined above; it is, rather, a statement about the 'Human Condition', and one in which the farcical absurdity of the human lot in the general scheme of things is made predominant. Satire, in this sense, partakes of both comedy and tragedy, but in itself it is neither. Hardy, of course, uses both these other terms extensively – for example, the subtitle of *Ethelberta* is *A Comedy in Chapters*, a short story is entitled 'A Tragedy of Two Ambitions', a poem 'A Tramp-woman's Tragedy'. But so, too, do the critics, who have traditionally applauded his 'rustic' comedy, and, even more to the point, as we have heard, his status as a tragic novelist: a Macmillan Casebook, indeed, is entitled *Hardy: The Tragic Novels*, as though there was no argument about it. However, if we listen to Hardy himself using the word 'tragedy', it usually sounds rather closer to the version of satire outlined above; for example: 'If you look beneath the surface of any farce you see a tragedy; and on the contrary, if you blind yourself to the deeper issues to a tragedy you see a farce' (*Life*, 215; see also the poem 'The Coquette, and After', l. 3, in Chapter 5); 'a tragedy exhibits a state of things in the life of an individual which unavoidably causes some natural aims or desire of his to end in a catastrophe when carried out' (*Life*, 176), and, of London:

> The people in this tragedy laugh, sing, smoke, toss off wines, etc., make love to girls in drawing-rooms and areas; and yet are playing their parts in the tragedy just the same. Some wear jewels and feathers, some wear rags. All are caged birds; the only difference lies in the size of the cage. This too is part of the tragedy. (*Life*, 171)

Nothing very heroic about all this – rather a mordant sense of what a later generation would label 'the Absurd'.

There is no space here to engage in a full-scale discussion of tragedy. What I propose to do instead is to substitute 'satire' for 'tragedy' as the appropriate term to describe Hardy's fiction, and to see how it works out in a general consideration of his novels, while pausing on occasion to look in more detail at specific examples. (Space also precludes similar treatment of his other extensive and important fictional corpus – the short stories – but my hypothesis is very evidently applicable there, too: think only of the titles of two volumes of such – *Life's Little Ironies* and *A Group of Noble Dames*). My two especial concerns will be (i) to bring out the novels' depiction of the 'satire' of sexual relationships in a class society; and (ii), perhaps more disturbingly, to expose Hardy's continual satire on the generic 'absolute falsity' (see above) of fictional discourse – in particular of that which purports to be 'telling things as they really are'. The second form of satire is, of course, the medium for realizing the first, although the larger impact of Hardy's fiction arguably lies in the negation of notions of 'making sense' of existence – either in life or in representation – which both aspects of satire together enact. Along the way, the appropriateness of using satire to define the fiction will be tested by seeing how it can accommodate *all* the novels, and all the elements *within* all the novels: how well it dispenses, in other words, with the need to excise 'flaws', to explain away 'awkwardnesses' and 'improbablities', and conveniently to lose sight of those troublesome 'minor' works.

I have no intention of flattening Hardy's fiction by suggesting that various inflexions of the 'poor-man-and-the-lady' theme everywhere pervade it. Nevertheless, it is difficult to ignore the fact – although many critics have successfully done so – that the plots, and much of the detail, pivot on cross-class relationships between male and female characters or, perhaps more exactly, relationships in which there is significant economic disparity. This is then overdetermined by the vast majority of the main characters, for one reason or another, being displaced from their 'true' class *locus*, being between classes, or being in the wrong place or community for their class type. In a passing phrase in

Ethelberta, Hardy speaks of the 'metamorphic classes of society' (*HE* 320). He thus exactly sums up the social group he focuses on – classes undergoing, as the dictionary puts it, 'complete transformation' – for most of his protagonists are indeed in transition, are in some way *déclassé* and *déraciné*, are undergoing some structural change in their social positioning. If tragedies (for which read satires) develop, it is not principally because 'Character is Destiny' (for more on this phrase, see below on *The Mayor of Casterbridge*) or because a cosmic Fate brings heroic individuals low; it is because the social order is rapidly changing and individuals on the move become involved with others also on the move, neither of whom have any familiar bearings or coordinates to navigate by. Such characters may be male or female, but, as an index of Hardy's acute societal intuition in the last half of the nineteenth century, many of the most 'metamorphic' and destabilizing characters are female: in some sense, he realized that shifts in the traditional class structure of society would be less seismic than upheavals in the patriarchal order. It is also apparent, without again factitiously transmuting all Hardy's fiction into a 'socialistic' discourse, that the 'satires of circumstance' in which most of these 'metamorphic' characters find themselves are the effects – not of Nemesis or of a personal *hamartia* – but of exploitation and dispossession as reflexes of economic (and related, legal) inequities and injustices. The satire may be articulated by 'absurd' instances of chance, coincidence, and contingency, but these are not its *cause*; rather, they are the telling representation of a social artifice which ruins human lives from behind a screen, 'realistically' depicting the current order, as natural, inevitable, and immutable. Tess's happening on the text-writer on her way home after losing her virginity to Alec d'Urberville may well appear 'improbable', but the presence in Hardy's text of the 'Crushing! Killing!' letters: THOU, SHALT, NOT, COMMIT –' (*T*. 96–7) graphically *represents* the 'satire' of her economic and sexual exploitation in a speciously Christian society.

Right from the start, Hardy's published novels are centred on and obsessed by class relations and their minutiae – especially those involving 'metamorphic' individuals. It is worth noting, for instance, that, apart from Geraldine Allenville in 'An Indiscretion in the Life of an Heiress' and Viviette, Lady Constantine, in *Two on a Tower*, there are no true 'ladies' in

Hardy's full-length fiction – all those in superior social positions having had these thrust upon them in one way or another. In *Desperate Remedies*, the spring of the plot is the secret personal connection between Cytherea – from a good professional background, but left penniless when her bankrupt architect father dies – and the 'lady' squire, Miss Aldclyffe, who employs her as a 'lady's-maid' ('Such a disgrace...', says her equally penurious architect-student brother (*DR* 84). But it is the following kind of gratuitous detail about Miss Aldclyffe's lineage – contributing absolutely nothing to the plot – which bears witness to the matrix in which Hardy's novels are shaped:

> 'Her family is a branch of the old Aldclyffe family on the maternal side. Her mother married a Bradleigh – a mere nobody at that time – and was on that account cut by her relations. But very singularly the other branch of the family died out one by one – three of them, and Miss Aldclyffe's great-uncle then left all his property, including this estate, to Captain Bradleigh and his wife – Miss Aldclyffe's father and mother – on condition that they took the old family name as well. There's all about it in the *Landed Gentry*.' (*DR* 109)

Equally, Cytherea's young lover, whom she finally marries after the death of her first husband (and by way of whom her children will one day inherit Miss Aldclyffe's estate), is both a Hardy-like architect's clerk and 'thorough artist, but a man of rather humble origin... the son of a farmer, or something of the kind' (*DR* 57). He too, however, has to make his career and does not initially have the money to marry, the novel commenting with satirical sententiousness (and echoing the famous opening of *Pride and Prejudice*?): 'It is a melancholy truth for the middle classes, that ... the man who works up a good income has had no time to learn love to its solemn extreme; the man who has learnt that has had no time to get rich' (*DR* 79). His father is indeed a farmer – but of an interesting kind: he is actually the landlord of an ancient coaching inn in a village which stands on 'one of the great highways in this part of England'. However – the novel informs us – 'the railway had absorbed the whole stream of traffic which formerly flowed through the village... reducing the empty-handed landlord... to the necessity of eking out his attenuated income by increasing the extent of his agricultural business if he would still maintain his social standing' (*DR* 153). The Springroves, in other words, are very clearly part of the transition of English social life in the mid-nineteenth century – a transition underscored by another significant event which affects them. Mr Springrove the elder – like Giles Winterbourne in the later 'major' Wessex novel, *The Woodlanders,* who, as we shall see, is centrally caught up in the 'metamorphic' social process too (they are also both cider-makers and the cider-making scenes are described very similarly) – is dispossessed by the lease on his property falling in and reverting to his landlord, the lady-squire, Miss Aldclyffe (in Giles's case, to the *arriviste* 'lady', Felice Charmond; see below).

Such preoccupations continue throughout the novels. Elfride Swancourt, the heroine of *A Pair of Blue Eyes,* is the daughter of a rural clergyman and has pretensions to a literary career. Her young lover, Stephen Smith, is the son of 'a cottager and a working master-mason'; and we are told his mother's people 'had been well-to-do yeoman for centuries, but she was only a dairy-maid, having been left an orphan' (*PBE* 104–5). The forebears of Lord Luxellian, whom Elfride marries 'for the benefit of my family' (*PBE* 400) – this, and her subsequent sudden death, are the dramatically late dénouement of the novel – were 'hedgers and ditchers by rights', whose elevation to the aristocracy is told in an absurdly comic scene (ch. 2). Lord Luxellian himself is at one point described by the novel as resembling 'a good-natured commercial traveller of the superior class' (*PBE* 170). In the popular bucolic pastoral, *Under the Greenwood Tree,* Fancy Day is nevertheless very precisely class-positioned as the daughter of a superior rural worker – 'head game keeper, timber steward, and general over-looker for this district' on the Earl of Wessex's estates (*UGT* 110); but she has also been 'in training' and is now the village schoolmistress (*UGT* 46). Both Hardy's sister and his cousin, Tryphena Sparks, also attended teacher training college, and the development of the profession of primary-school teaching in the nineteenth century was centrally instrumental in the upward social mobility of lower-class young women. Fancy has, once again, strong affinities with Grace Melbury in *The Woodlanders,* as indeed have Mr Melbury and Fancy's father, Geoffrey, who, until comically persuaded otherwise, rejects the local carrier's son Dick Dewey's proposal of marriage to her on strict and specific class grounds. Having outlined in proud detail the process and accomplishments of Fancy's betterment, he asks the impecunious Dick why he thinks he (Geoffrey) lives 'in such a miserly way', and gives the answer himself: 'That if any gentleman, who sees her to be his equal in polish, should want to marry her, and she want to marry him, he shan't be superior to her in pocket. Now do ye think after this that you be good enough for her?' (*UGT* 166–7). Indeed, the only cloud to pass over this romantic pastoral idyll is when the 'polished' returned native, Fancy, momentarily agrees to marry Parson Maybold – the other 'outsider' in this rural community – bewitched principally by the fact that, unlike Dick, he carries an umbrella 'of superior silk – less common at that date than since – and of elegant make' (*UGT* 182). In response to his proposal – and anticipating later 'satires' of a darker hue – Fancy agitatedly whispers: 'the temptation is, O, too strong, and I can't resist it' (*UGT* 184). In this still comic world, however, she does.

And so the detailed weaving of the social fabric goes on. Bathsheba Everdene, in Hardy's first major success, *Far from the Madding Crowd* – a second, if rather more troubled, pastoral – is also precisely delineated as a metamorphic outsider. Daughter of a bankrupt 'gentleman-tailor really' ('of a higher circle of life'), and herself 'an excellent scholar [who] was going to be a governess once' – the main profession in the earlier nineteenth century for poor genteel females (*FMC* 74, 47) – she inherits her uncle's farm and becomes that rare anomaly at the time, a female farmer. Her relations with the male characters indicate just how disruptive a figure she is seen to be: early on rejecting the yeoman farmer, Gabriel Oak, she is courted by and marries the itinerant soldier, Sergeant Troy ('a fairly well-educated man for one of middle class – exceptionally well-educated for a common soldier' (*FMC* 157; see also 155): note how Hardy never misses the exact class coordinate), in the process also fuelling the disastrous passion of the 'gentleman-farmer', Mr Boldwood. In the end, the pastoral mode triumphs with Bathsheba and Gabriel married, but 'satire' has come uncomfortably close.

For many critics and readers, it is everywhere uncomfortably present in Hardy's next novel, *The Hand of Ethelberta*, which, *The Life* significantly tells us, gave him 'the satisfaction of proving, amid the general disappointment at the lack of sheep and shepherds, that he did not mean to imitate anybody' (*Life*, 103). This does not sound like a writer committed to pastoral Wessex; and indeed *Ethelberta* is the most overtly metropolitan and fictively self-reflexive class satire of all Hardy's works. Space forbids extended analysis of this complex novel here,[5] although a passage illustrating its self-conscious fictional display is analysed below. Suffice to say that Ethelberta, whose family are servants and workmen, fashions herself into a 'lady', enters 'good' society in London – most of which is shown to be as factitious as she is (one country estate is founded on 'a very large fortune by the knacker business and tanning' whose owners 'live like lords' and who are called Neigh! (*HE* 200)) – and eschews her young 'poor-man' lover in favour of marrying the wicked old aristocrat, Lord Mountclere. Much of her career has depended, as we heard earlier, on her success as a 'professed romancer' – telling 'fictional' stories about herself as though they were true (which, in fact, they are). Postmodern self-reflexivity would find this a hard act to follow.

But let us see how this self-consciously fictive novel itself foregrounds the artifice of its own fictionality, and, in so doing, at the same time discloses the artificiality of the class system itself as a socially divisive fiction. To perceive this trope at work may then act as a monitory guide to how we should position ourselves in reading *all* Hardy's fiction. Chapter Twenty-Nine depicts a dinner party at the London home of Mr and Mrs Doncastle, where Ethelberta's father is the butler, and where Ethelberta – as the well-connected widow, Mrs Petherwin – is to dine. None of her Society acquaintances, of course, knows of her 'real' background, nor that she is the butler's daughter – indeed, much of the novel's plot is entailed with keeping all this secret. Ethelberta's sister, Picotee, who is herself passed off as Ethelberta's maid, has wanted to see her 'sitting at a grand dinner-table, among lordly dishes and shining people, and father about the room unnoticed!' (*HE*, ch. 28, p. 223; we may notice in passing Hardy's slyly ironic inversion of adjectives here: for it is the dishes which are 'lordly' and the people 'shining' – with their new and meretricious 'polish' – rather than the other way round). It is arranged that Picotee will secretly observe the scene:

> Through the partly-opened door there became visible a sideboard which first attracted her attention by its richness. It was, indeed, a noticeable example of modern art-workmanship, in being exceptionally large, with curious ebony mouldings at different stages; and, while the heavy cupboard doors at the bottom were enriched with inlays of paler wood, other panels were decorated with tiles, as if the massive composition had been erected on the spot as part of the solid building. However, it was on a space higher up that Picotee's eyes and thoughts were fixed. In the great mirror above the middle ledge she could see reflected the upper part of the dining-room, and this suggested to her that she might see Ethelberta and the other guests reflected in the same way by standing on a chair, which, quick as thought, she did.
>
> To Picotee's dazed young vision her beautiful sister appeared as the chief figure of a glorious pleasure parliament of both sexes, surrounded by whole regiments of candles grouped here and there about the room. She and her companions were seated before a large flower-bed, or small hanging garden, fixed at about the level of the elbow, the attention of all being concentrated rather upon the uninteresting margin of the bed, and upon each other, than on the beautiful natural objects growing in the middle, as it seemed to Picotee. In the ripple of conversation Ethelberta's clear voice could occasionally be heard, and her young sister could see that her eyes were bright, and her face beaming, as if divers social wants and looming penuriousness had never been within her experience. Mr Doncastle was quite absorbed in what she was saying. So was the queer old man whom Menlove had called Lord Mountclere.
>
> 'The dashing widow looks very well, does she not?' said a person at Picotee's elbow. (*HE* 233)

We immediately register the opulence of the furniture, especially that 'noticeable example of modern art-workmanship', the sideboard: its 'exceptional' size; its 'curious ebony mouldings' (where 'curious' can mean 'finely-worked' or 'intricate', but also 'odd', 'extraordinary'); its various other eclectic decorative features; and its massive solidity – all of which encodes its showy *nouveau-riche* bad taste. What is less obvious is that Hardy surely has in mind the Veneerings in Dickens's *Our Mutual Friend,* those wonderfully 'bran-new people in a bran-new house in a bran-new quarter of London', who also own a sideboard: 'The great looking-glass above the sideboard, reflects the table and the company. Reflects the new Veneering crest, in gold and eke in silver. . . '.[6] By this artful intertextual reference, Hardy reinforces the specious artificiality of the new middle and upper classes. This is compounded by the description of the dinner party proper. The grandiosely overstated image of 'a glorious pleasure-parliament... surrounded by whole regiments of candles' parallels, in its bombastic grandiloquence, the excessive extravagance of the hosts and their guests – a trope repeated in the hyperbolic absurdity of the table decoration: 'a large flower-bed or small hanging-garden'. Notice, too, that the company are more interested in 'each other' than in 'the beautiful *natural* objects' (emphasis added) of the display. In the midst of all this sits Ethelberta, 'the chief figure' in the scene, her 'clear voice', 'bright' eyes, and 'beaming' face, in fact, of course, part of her *performance* as a well-to-do, well-bred 'lady' – a performance disguising – as the text in a sudden serious modulation is quick to remind us – 'divers social wants and looming penuriousness'. Indeed, throughout the novel, the mask-like reification of Ethelberta's face is reiterated – as though she lives her real life behind it, while it becomes a sign of her falsity and alienation; for example: 'The face of Ethelberta showed caution at once' (*HE* 94); 'the face of Ethelberta showed venturesomeness' (*HE* 94); 'Ethelberta smiled a smile of many meanings' (*HE* 41); 'But none of this reached her face' (*HE* 314). All this is brought together, in the present passage, by the final comment of Picotee's 'conductor': 'The dashing widow looks very well...' 'Dashing widow' itself combines two contradictory terms – with the flashy brilliance of 'dashing' reminding us of the 'shining people' earlier – but 'looks very well' is more subtle. The phrase can mean 'in good health' and also that she 'looks good' (i.e. beautiful or well-turned-out); but in this context, it also at once focuses attention on her *appearance* (of being a 'lady') and on the sense in which 'looks' implies 'seems' – that is, 'looks' something she is not. Much earlier in the novel there is a wonderfully ironic sentence which may act as a gloss on the present one: '[her] appearance answer[ing] as fully as ever to that of an English Lady skilfully perfected in manner, carriage, *look* and accent' (*HE* 113; emphasis added). It is difficult to know whether that phrase denoting premeditated and rehearsed artifice – 'skilfully perfected' – refers to Ethelberta's 'appearance' (her 'look') or to the generic 'English Lady's'. Such sentences are, indeed, characteristic of Hardy's layered prose – if we read it with care.

'Looks very well', however, also reminds us that the most contrived and self-conscious feature of the passage is the way *it* and *we* are 'looking', too. The dinner party, and Ethelberta centrally, are 'seen' by way of a complex set of voyeuristic displacements: the 'partly-opened door' allows Picotee to peep into the dining room and see the sideboard on which the 'great mirror' reflects the guests, but it is only by climbing on a chair that she can see them, with Ethelberta as 'chief figure'. We too, as readers, let us be clear, also only 'see' Ethelberta – reflected in a mirror – by being balanced on that chair and through the gap in the doorway. But in *our own seeing* of this manner of 'seeing' we may come to realize how the scene formally enacts, in its own presentational strategies, the deception and alienation of a class system, which the whole novel – and, I would argue, most of Hardy's others – exposes. Not only are Picotee and the father/butler dissociated from their own relative by the 'fiction' of class position, but Ethelberta herself has become no more than an image displaced in a mirror and seen obliquely through a half-open door. This, however, is very much her 'reality'; she is indeed (false) 'appearance', 'performance', 'look', contrived and exposed in the self-displaying fictiveness of the discourses which, at the same time, constitute and claim her as 'real' – those of the novel itself. Our theatre-like positioning as observers of the performance here should, in the other (Brechtian) sense of 'alienation', make us simultaneously 'see' both the performance and that it *is* performance. If we take the hint, much of Hardy's other fiction will release markedly similar strategies of looking and seeing.

This obtrusively artificial *Comedy in Chapters* – a subtitle itself sufficiently self-conscious – was succeeded by Hardy's first explicitly Wessex novel, the 'tragic' *The Return of the Native.* However, if we focus less exclusively on Egdon Heath as universal backdrop or on the high passion of Eustacia, Clym, and Wildeve, it is clearly evident that a similar pattern of class relations and 'metamorphic' individuals is the structuring framework of this book, as it is in other novels. Clym's mother, whose aspirations for her son are the mainspring of the plot, is 'a curate's daughter who had once dreamt of doing better things', although in the event she had married only 'a small farmer' (*RN*

54). Clym, of course, like so many of Hardy's protagonists, has been educated to a level which separates him off from his home community; becomes a 'manager to a diamond merchant' in Paris (*RN* 116); and returns – the disillusioned 'native' – to keep a school on Egdon in order to educate, in their turn, *its* natives (*RN* 170). Wildeve, who is now the landlord of an inn on the heath, has been an engineer 'in an office in Budmouth' (*RN* 61) – 'a clever, learned fellow . . . brought up to better things' (*RN* 46); and Eustacia Vye, whose 'native place' is really Budmouth, is one of the most hybrid of Hardy's main characters: the child of a 'Corfiote' bandmaster and the daughter of a sea-captain 'of good family' (*RN* 83). But it is the remarkable chapter VII, 'Queen of Night', which establishes Eustacia's disruptive character in terms at once sympathetic and subtly ironic: 'eternally unreconciled' to the heath on which she is constrained to live – 'she felt like one banished; but here she was forced to abide' (*RN* 82) – she shows 'smouldering rebelliousness' (*RN* 82–3), 'social nonconformity' (*RN* 85), and 'depression of spirits' (*RN* 86); she desires a 'blaze of love' (*RN* 84) and 'to be loved to madness' (*RN* 84); 'she desired it as one in a desert would be thankful for brackish water' (*RN* 84). It is perhaps the sly bathos of that last image which suggests that satire rather than high tragedy is what we are to witness here (the chapter has opened with the ambivalent statement: 'Eustacia Vye was the raw material of a divinity', and the prose continues throughout to leave the reader uncertain as to whether it is earnest or sardonic). The novel's complex sociological narrative – in which a number of inorganic individuals come into contact with each other in an alien environment – is presented as a series of ironic mistakes inevitably determined by the flawed vision of people whose aspirations are without firm social bearings. The essentially *petit bourgeois* romantic, Eustacia, misperceives Clym as her ticket to a cosmopolitan life; Clym is – in the end, literally – blind both to her desires and to the hopeless idealism of his own ambitions; Wildeve, against his better judgement, is mechanically drawn back to Eustacia time after time; Mrs Yeobright's ambitions for Clym end in her death – brought about by an 'improbable' combination of coincidences. And so on. But it is as much the *manner* in which all this is treated as the action itself which illustrates how the novel subjects to satire its own apparently most serious components. Three examples will suffice. The final description of its 'tragic' heroine reads: 'The stateliness of look which had been almost too marked for a dweller in a country domicile had at least found an artistically happy background' (*RN* 339) – bathetic phrasing which surely undercuts any tragic status the drowned Eustacia may have had. Secondly, of Clym's new career as 'itinerant open-air preacher and lecturer on morally unimpeachable subjects' – and we may recall the later grotesque satire on Alec d'Urberville in a similar guise (*T.*, chs. XLV–VI) – the novel's penultimate sentence wryly tells us: 'while others again remarked that it was well enough for a man to take to preaching who could not see to do anything else' (*RN* 364–5). Finally, at the end of the preceding chapter (Book Sixth, III), which indicates that Thomasin is indeed going to marry Diggory Venn, Hardy appends a footnote:

> The writer may state here that the original conception of the story did not design a marriage between Thomasin and Venn.... But certain circumstances of serial publication led to a change of intent.
>
> Readers can therefore choose between the endings, and those with an austere artistic code can assume the more consistent conclusion to be the true one. (*RN* 356).

What on earth did Hardy mean? The note was added to the 'Wessex Edition' in 1912, which, of course, reprints the existing 'happy' ending: so which *is* 'the more consistent conclusion'? Hardy does not say; but my feeling is that 'those with an austere artistic code' – note the phrasing once more – who elect for the more 'tragic' one are themselves being subjected to Hardy's satire.

Even in his next novel, the popular comic pastoral, *The Trumpet-Major* – set in Wessex in the period of the Napoleonic Wars – the plot of the romance is based on cross-class sexual relationships between characters whose social position is unstable. Both the sons of Miller Loveday are in love with Anne Garland, the genteel but 'reduced' daughter of 'a landscape painter's widow' – 'two ladies of good report, though unfortunately of limited means' (*TM* 27). The Lovedays are 'an ancient family of corn-grinders' who had 'formed matrimonial alliances with farmers not so very small, and once with a gentleman-farmer' but who were derived from 'the rank known as ceorls or villeins, full of importance to the country at large, and ramifying throughout the unwritten history of England' (*TM* 33–4; note once more Hardy's exact specificity of social location). Both sons, however, are very much of the 'metamorphic' mould – one is a musician major in the dragoons, the other a 'sailor-miller' (*TM* 37). But it is in the following two novels, *A Laodicean*, one of the most despised of the 'minor' works, and *Two on a Tower* – both, let us be clear, well into the Wessex phase of Hardy's fiction – that the 'poor-man-and-the-lady' theme, along with other now familiar class complexities, re-emerges in inescapably satiric form.

We will look in detail at an example of the self-consciously mannered discourse of *A Laodicean* in a moment, but I have space here[7] only to state that the degree and intrusiveness of the sensationalism, melodrama, comic absurdity, and overwrought style of much of the novel convince me, at least, that this is satire at a number of levels – not least directed at the factitious discourses of fictional writing itself, and especially those of a realism which claims veracity (we may think, for example, of George Eliot's invocation of 'this rare, precious quality of truthfulness' in asserting her intention of giving 'a faithful account', of seeking 'the exact truth', in *Adam Bede*, ch. XVII). *A Laodicean* is expressly concerned with the 'clash between ancient and modern' (*L.* 62) – a phrase it inflects more than once (e.g. 'the turmoil between ancient and modern' (*L.* 345)) – and, equally clearly if less explicitly, 'the incongruities that were daily shaping themselves in the world under the great modern fluctuations of classes and creeds'(*L.* 67). It would be hard to find a more exact and synoptic definition of Hardy's 'satire' – throughout all his fiction – than 'the incongruities... shaping themselves.... under the great modern fluctuations of classes and creeds' . Paula Power, the novel's heroine, is the daughter of a (late) 'great railway contractor', MP, and 'great Nonconformist' (*L.* 62); she has inherited an ancient estate which her father had bought, and is now the owner of a castle and its contents once owned by displaced old aristocrats, the De Stancys. In other words, Paula *Power* (her name is significant) is a 'lady', but only by way of 'new money'; in this, she is one of that entrepreneurial class of estate-owning *arrivistes* (Power without responsibility perhaps) which also includes Alfred Neigh in

Ethelberta, Felice Charmond in *The Woodlanders*, and Alec d'Urberville in *Tess* (indeed, Paula's entire 'romantic' relationship with the De Stancys is based on an inversion of the established class hierarchies – she has bought their heredity – and is closely analogous to Alec's predatory one with the Durbeyfields – he has bought theirs). It is Paula's courtship by William De Stancy, the 'true' soldier-heir, on the one hand, and, on the other, by the 'poor-man' trainee-architect George Somerset, of professional middle-class background (his father is a society painter), which comprises the novel's plot. Significantly, in this case, it is the latter who forms the 'alliance' with the 'new aristocrat' (*L.* 429), Paula, at the end (although her castle has been burnt to the ground); but he has, nevertheless, felt her 'social position as a woman of wealth... a perceptible bar' (*L.* 341) to his wooing of her, and – strikingly explicit in our present context – explains his 'delicacy' in asking for her hand by remarking 'the woman is rich, and the man is poor' (*L.* 422).

However, as I have said, Hardy's satire here is primarily apparent in the self-revealing display of fictional devices, motifs, and mannerisms in a novel which is itself packed with images of (mis)representation: from the (dubiously) 'true reflections of their prototypes' (*L.* 55) in the De Stancy ancestral portraits to the productions of William De Stancy's illegitimate son, William Dare, the melodrama-villain photographer, who, while 'contriving to produce what seemed to be a perfect likeness' (*L.* 332), in fact produces a totally false one. In this, the inference we may draw is that Dare resembles the realist novelist (Defoe, Ethelberta) whose tales have 'the one pre-eminent merit of seeming like truth', and yet, in fact, are 'absolutely false', 'utterly untrue' (see the discussion of *The Hand of Ethelberta*, earlier).

As an illustration of the self-conscious fictionality of Hardy's writing here, let us look in detail at a passage which, like the one from *Ethelberta* above, again brings sharply into view both his narrative positioning of the reader as complicit in the alienated *looking at* of a character and his mannered ironic style – this time with heavily charged sexual undertones. The scene, in Book II Chapter VII, has been described by one critic of Hardy's 'lesser novels' as 'the most widely mocked'[8] of the novel's unintended comic absurdities. 'Mocked' it may have been by critics concerned to read Hardy as a wayward and 'flawed' realist genius, but whether the comic absurdity is *unintended* remains to be seen. William Dare has arranged for his 'dad' to see the lovely heiress, Paula Power, so that he will be seduced away from his self-imposed vow of fidelity to his dead lover (Dare's mother), pay court to Paula, marry her, and thus restore the family to its rightful inheritance (the castle, etc.). Paula is working out in her modern gym deep in the woods, entirely unconscious that she is being spied upon; Dare has engineered a hole in the gym wall through which can be seen 'quite a curiosity, and really worth seeing' (*L.* 196); De Stancy moves forward, now slightly the worse for drink – which, the text obligingly tells us, 'would have been *comical to an outsider*' (*L.* 196; emphases added, and throughout the passage which follows):

> and *looked through the hole into the interior* of the gymnasium. Dare withdrew to some little distance, and *watched* Captain De Stancy's face, which presently began to assume an expression of interest.
>
> What was the captain *seeing*? A sort of *optical poem*.
>
> Paula, in a pink flannel costume, was bending, wheeling, and undulating in the air *like a gold-fish in its globe*, sometimes ascending by her arms nearly to the lantern, then lowering herself till she swung level with the floor. Her aunt Mrs Goodman, and Charlotte De Stancy, were sitting on campstools at one end, *watching* her gyrations, Paula occasionally addressing them with such an expression as – 'Now, Aunt, *look at me* – and you, Charlotte – is not that shocking to your weak nerves', when some adroit feat would be repeated, which, however, seemed to give much more pleasure to Paula herself in *performing* it than to Mrs Goodman in *looking on*, the latter sometimes saying, 'Oh, it is terrific – do not run such a risk again!'
>
> It would have demanded the poetic passion of some joyous Elizabethan lyrist like Lodge, Nashe, or Greene, to fitly phrase Paula's *presentation of herself* at this moment of absolute abandonment to every muscular whim that could take possession of such a supple form. The white manilla ropes clung about *the performer* like snakes as she took her exercise, and the colour in her face deepened as she went on. Captain De Stancy felt that, much as he had *seen* in early life of beauty in woman, he had never *seen* beauty of such a real and living sort as this. A bitter recollection of his vow, together with a sense that *to gaze* on the festival of this Bona Dea was, though so innocent and *pretty a sight*, hardly fair or gentlemanly, would have compelled him to *withdraw his eyes*, had not the sportive fascination

> of *her appearance glued them there* in spite of all. And as if to complete *the picture* of Grace personified and add the one thing wanting to the charm which bound him, the clouds, till that time thick in the sky, broke away from the upper heaven, and allowed the noonday sun to pour down through *the lantern* upon her, *irradiating* her with a warm light that was incarnadined by her pink doublet and hose, and *reflected in* upon her face. She only required a cloud to rest on instead of the green silk net which actually supported her reclining figure for the moment, to be quite *Olympian*; save indeed that in place of haughty effrontery there *sat on her countenance* only the healthful sprightliness of an English girl....
>
> To *precisely describe* Captain De Stancy's *look* ['admiration' in some versions] was impossible. A sun seemed to rise in his face. By *watching* him they could almost *see the aspect of her* within the wall, so accurately were her changing phases *reflected in* him. He seemed to forget that he was not alone.
>
> 'And is this,' he murmured, in the manner of one only half apprehending himself, 'and is this the end of my vow?'
>
> Paula was saying at this moment, 'Ariel sleeps in *this posture*, does he not, Auntie?' Suiting the action to the word, she flung out her arms behind her head as she lay in the green silk hammock, idly *closed her pink eyelids*, and swung herself to and fro. (*L*. 196–8)

In the Victorian context, as also in our jaded own, the scene is inescapably erotically charged: at once in its celebration of Paula's potent physical sexuality – even if innocent in itself – and, conversely, in its corrupting of that innocence by the scopophilic framing of it by what we would now call 'the male gaze' (my emphases will have drawn attention, amongst other things, to the passage's iteration of words and phrases to do with 'looking' and 'picturing'). That Hardy was fully conscious of the eroticism of the passage is evidenced by the revisions he made to it in the various versions of the novel. For example, Paula's costume in the serial publication uncompromisingly 'showed to perfection every curve of her figure', a clause deleted in the book edition; where the book version has, as here, 'shocking to your weak nerves', the serial has Paula saying 'is not that pretty'; the 1896 book edition added 'innocent and', as here, to the serial's 'though so pretty'; conversely, where the serial had 'strange fascination', the book changed the adjective to 'sportive', as here, with its connotations of being 'roguish', 'wanton', 'amorous'. Furthermore, it does not take an especially prurient mind to register the overt sexuality of the whole description: Paula is 'bending... and undulating'; is giving way to '*absolute abandonment to every muscular whim* that could *take possession* of such a *supple form*' (emphases added); the 'white manilla ropes' cling about her 'like snakes'; 'the colour in her face deepened as she went on'; 'Bona Dea' (literally 'the good goddess') is the Roman goddess of chastity – but also of fertility – who was worshipped only by women, although, by an erotic inversion, not so here; the spectacle should have compelled De Stancy to '*withdraw* his eyes', but Paula's 'sportive' appearance '*glued* them there in spite of all' (emphases added); the sun 'pouring down' through the 'lantern' (both skylight and, suggestively, an early film projector) bathes her in a kind of artificial lighting: 'irradiating her with a warm light that was incarnadined by her pink doublet and hose, and reflected in upon her face' – 'incarnadine' means having the pinkish colour *of flesh*, and pink, especially in Hardy's poetry, invariably signals the erotic.

Consider, too, the physical implications of Paula's tightly pink-clad figure, either with ropes clinging 'like snakes' round her 'supple form' or 'reclining' (i.e. lying on her back) 'supported' by a 'green silk net': our contemporary soft-porn photographers (and let us not forget that William Dare is one of the earliest photographers in English fiction) could scarcely dream up a more explicit way of exhibiting female flesh. But the following word 'Olympian', beyond its surface sense of 'goddess-like', may also invoke Manet's nearly contemporary (1865) sensual painting of a courtesan, 'Olympia', who is also reclining nude on a bed, with one hand prudishly but provocatively lying over her pudendum – a painting which had been a *succès de scandale* when first exhibited.[9] Leaving aside the 'sun ris[ing] in [De Stancy's] face', and the poor man's inability to 'withdraw' his eyes which are 'glued' to Paula's 'body', we may conclude this account of the passage's visual erotic fantasy by noting Paula's surely auto-orgasmic 'posture' in the final lines: 'she flung out her arms behind her head as she lay in the green silk hammock, idly closed her pink eyelids, and swung herself to and fro'. This is a late-Victorian centrefold in all but name.

However, it is also noteworthy that the language of the passage, on two occasions in particular, draws attention to the theatricality of Paula's display in a scene which is itself inescapably theatrical. First there is 'Paula's *presentation of herself* at this moment of absolute abandonment', and then, just below – with the ropes clinging around her – she is called 'the performer' (earlier she is also described as 'performing' one of her feats). This, together with De Stancy's viewing position in the first line of the passage, is surely not a fortuitous, *unintended* invocation of the 'peep-show' – of 'What the Butler Saw'? Other evidence in the passage also points to a high degree of self-consciously arch alienation in the narrative stance and style. We have noted in passing above how Dare 'frames' the scene by calling it 'quite a curiosity', and how De Stancy is burlesqued as potentially 'comical to an outsider'; but in answer to its own stylized question as to what the captain was 'seeing', the narrative answers with the equally mannered and self-reflexive phrase: 'a sort of optical poem' – which offers a definition not only of the scene in the gym but also of the novel's own *representation* of that scene. Later, the passage grandiloquently invokes 'the poetic passion of some joyous Elizabethan lyrist' (note the oddity of the word – not 'lyr*ic*ist') in pretending to avow its own inadequacy for the task of doing justice to the scene. Similarly, it draws attention to its own descriptive incapacity when it claims that 'to precisely describe Captain De Stancy's look was impossible' (note, as in the *Ethelberta* passage analysed earlier, the ambiguity of the word 'look': both his appearance and his 'look*ing*' – his transfixed male 'gaze'); and the passage further undercuts itself by a kind of mock-heroic bathos when Paula, requiring 'only ... a cloud to rest on ... to be quite Olympian', is brought suddenly to earth instead by being described as exuding 'only the healthful sprightliness of an English girl'.

Finally, we may note that the present scene has an overt negative analogue in an earlier chapter (Bk I, Ch. II), where George's '*gaze* into the lighted chapel' (*L.* 45; emphasis added) sees the recusant Paula, this time 'clothed in an ample robe of flowing white' (*L.* 46), refuse to enter the baptismal pool – and so, we must assume, *fail to see* the clinging wet robe reveal her 'supple form'. For George, 'there was but one scene: the *imagined scene* of the girl herself as she sat alone in the vestry' (*L.* 49; emphasis added). The fact that the erotically realized Paula-in-the-gym episode so closely parallels and inverts this chaste, sexually repressed, and 'imagined' scene as surely further evidence, if any were needed, that we are in the presence of highly self-reflexive composition in this novel and of writing which is very conscious of the artifice of fiction. Whether we see the narrative stance in the gym passage as finally complicit in the eroticized fantasy of the male gaze or as ironically subverting it is a moot point – as it is with the similarly erotic presentation of Tess in the later novel. What seems to me incontrovertible here, however, is that any 'comic absurdity' is directed towards the reader – especially (male) ones who do not get the joke.

In the retrospective Preface (1895) to *Two on a Tower*, Hardy notes that, on the novel's first publication in 1882, 'people' took it that 'it was intended to be a *satire* on the Established Church of this country' (emphasis added) – a phrase which will bring to mind the description of *The Poor Man and the Lady* quoted earlier. Given that *Two on a Tower* is principally concerned with the relationship between Viviette, Lady Constantine, the widow of Sir Blount Constantine of ancient family – the only true 'lady' in all of Hardy's full-length fiction – and Swithin St Cleeve, a young astronomer who is the son of an erratic curate and a farmer's daughter (and therefore a type of 'the poor man'), we should attend to Hardy's prefatory remarks with interest. It is striking, then, that nowhere does he deny the charge of a satire on the church, remarking only that 'the Bishop [of "Melchester", whom Viviette finally marries] is every inch a gentleman', and that 'the pages must speak for themselves'. The pages do indeed 'speak for themselves', the Bishop being uncompromisingly presented as an unsufferably pompous, self-important prig. For example: 'the Bishop's words disclosed a mind whose sensitive fear of danger to its own dignity hindered it from criticism elsewhere' (*TT* 268); '"the advantages her mind would derive [he says] from the enlarged field of activity that the position of a bishop's wife would afford, are palpable"' (*TT* 270); 'Dr Helmsdale was standing there with the air of a man too good for his destiny – which, to be fair to him, was not far from the truth this time' (*TT* 272–3). Combined with the complex contingencies and ironies of the novel's plot in relation to the Viviette–Swithin romance, this overtly comic portrayal points to the satire of the whole work. On one occasion, for instance, Swithin is caught thinking thus: 'the glorious light of this tender and refined passion seemed to have become debased to burlesque hues by pure accident, and his aesthetic no less than his ethic taste was offended by such an anti-climax' (*TT* 206). 'Burlesque hues' and 'anti-climax' aptly describe a novel which ends with the once-more widowed Viviette, on hearing that Swithin has come back to marry her, uttering 'a shriek of amazed joy', and – rather like Elfride in *A Pair of Blue Eyes* – unexpectedly dying on the spot. The novel's final sentence is: 'The Bishop was avenged' (*TT* 291–2) – and the reader's 'aesthetic taste' thus strategically 'offended'.

Hardy himself saw his next novel, *The Mayor of Casterbridge*, as 'more particularly a study of one man's deeds and character' (1912 Preface) than any of the other Wessex novels, and criticism has certainly confirmed this in presenting Michael Henchard as *the* great tragic protagonist of Hardy's fiction. Without perversely wishing to reject this view out of hand, I would, nevertheless, ask the reader to reconsider *The Mayor* in the light of the signals identified so far in this chapter. Specificity of social class is once more very exact: Henchard, for example, was originally a hay-trusser whose work, the novel is at pains to insist, was that 'of the skilled countryman' as distinct from that of 'the general labourer' (*MC* 27). Farfrae has 'some inventions useful to the [corn] trade' (*MC* 61) – in other words, he is an engineer like Wildeve in *The Return of the Native*; Lucetta Templeman, like other female characters before her, is 'of good family, well bred and well educated': 'the daughter of some harum-scarum military officer who had got into difficulties' (*MC* 86), she has dropped into genteel poverty, only to inherit a sizeable fortune from a relative in Bristol which enables her to become 'the lady' of High-Place Hall, a mansion in the heart of Casterbridge. That she has changed her name to obscure her past, and that the narrative, in passing, associates her tenancy of the Hall with the old adage: 'Blood built it, and Wealth enjoys it' (*MC* 134), should not escape our attention. Clearly, this novel focuses once more on unstable 'metamorphic' individuals and outsiders who represent the tensions fostered by the transitions occurring within nineteenth-century class society: hay-trusser becomes prosperous corn merchant and mayor; Scottish 'new man', originally on his way to the New World, settles in Casterbridge; itinerant poor-genteel young woman becomes new-rich 'lady' of High-Place Hall. Furthermore, these individuals intersect in a solidly material society which is itself undergoing upheaval: Hardy is careful to point out, in the 1912 Preface, that the novel's action stems from the crisis in 'the home Corn Trade' – that is, 'the uncertain harvests which immediately preceded the repeal of the Corn Laws'. It is these which have put the younger Henchard out of work, and which account, too, for the 'pulling down' – rather than the building – of cottages for agricultural workers: 'there were five houses cleared away last year, and three this; and the volk nowhere to go...' (*MC* 29). Equally, it is worth noting the sympathetic terms in which the novel depicts Mixen Lane, the slum district of Casterbridge, from which emerges, pointedly, the terrifying 'burlesque' of the skimmity-ride which, as Bakhtinian Carnival, 'degrades' the pretensions of Henchard and Lucetta (she dies; he, grotesquely, sees his own effigy floating in the river):

> Yet amid so much that was bad needy respectability also found a home. Under some of the roofs abode pure and virtuous souls whose presence there was due to the iron hand of necessity, and to that alone. Families from decayed villages – families of that once bulky, but now nearly extinct, section of village society called 'liviers', or lifeholders – copyholders and others, whose roof-trees had fallen for some reason or other, compelling them to quit the rural spot that had been their home for generations – came here, unless they chose to lie under a hedge by the wayside. (*MC* 224)

The novel may, indeed, be *A Story of a Man of Character*, as the subtitle puts it, but Henchard's 'tragedy' is as much the result of social circumstances (poverty, injustice, capitalist economics, *change*) as it is of Fate or any *hamartia* in his 'Character'. Indeed, when reading the novel, and despite all the critical claims about it, I always find it difficult – if not impossible – to identify from the text precisely what that defect is supposed to be. Like George Eliot before him, Hardy may write: 'Character is Fate, said Novalis', and cast Henchard as a kind of latter-day Faust, but he makes it emphatically clear, too, that it is the 'trade-antagonism', the 'mortal commercial combat' with Farfrae, which determines his 'destiny' (*MC* 114–15). All human beings, in some sense, have 'Character', but it is the 'satires of circumstance' which constitute their 'Fate'. Perhaps the full title of Hardy's novel, in all its prosaic flatness – *The Life and Death of the Mayor of Casterbridge: A Story of a Man of Character* – is after all ironic, since Henchard is no more than an ordinary man (of susceptible character, like the rest of us) buffeted by the winds of change.

Similar characteristics traverse the texts of Hardy's last four novels: cross-class sexual relations; unstable and displaced individuals; satire at once circumstantial and formally inscribed in the self-conscious artifice and 'burlesque' of their very textuality. Of all Hardy's later fiction, with the possible exception of *Tess*, *The Woodlanders* – bearing that most pastoral-sounding of titles – can easily be regarded as the acme of his true stock-in-trade: set in the very heart of Wessex; epitomizing the 'Novels of Character and Environment'; a tragic love story; and a threnody for the passing of a traditional rural way of life. But to see it exclusively in such terms is to miss much of its social and satiric force. If we begin to gather up the characteristic social types which populate Hardy's fictional world, we find that, with the odd exception, they are all present in *The Woodlanders*: 'poor men' of the 'intermediate' class – the skilled life-holders and copy-holders of the rural economy (Farmer Springrove, Gabriel Oak, Diggory Venn, Jude Fawley – here, Giles Winterbourne); self-made men – especially with 'educated' daughters (Geoffrey Day, Henchard – here, Mr Melbury); factitious gentry – and especially 'ladies' – usually based on 'new money' (Alfred Neigh, Alec d'Urberville, Paula Power, Ethelberta, Lucetta – here, Felice Charmond/Grace Melbury); intelligent and sensitive lower-class women (Thomasin, Tess – here, Marty South); sexually active and socially unstable country women (Arabella – here, Suke Damson); displaced professional men (Farfrae, Wildeve, Clym, Sergeant Troy, Angel Clare – here, Fitzpiers); young women in part educated above their station (Tess, Sue Bridehead, Fancy Day, Eustacia, Ethelberta – here, Grace Melbury). In other words, this remote rural community is, by and large, composed of the most comprehensively 'metamorphic' group of individuals in all Hardy's fiction, and it is, of course, on their socio-sexual interrelationships that the novel pivots.

In this context, we should be alert once more to the exact specificity of the class location Hardy gives his characters. Giles Winterbourne is a life-holder, a woodsman and cider-maker whose skills are fast becoming redundant, and who is in a loose but inferior partnership with Mr Melbury. The latter is 'the chief man of business hereabout... the timber, bark and copse-ware merchant' (*W.* 35); he is 'of the sort called self-made, and had worked hard' (*W.* 47); he sends his daughter away to boarding school, 'at the figure of near a hundred a year' (*W.* 32), in part to alleviate his shame at his own lack of education; and he is acutely conscious of her elevated social status as a result: 'your sphere ought not to be middling' (*W.* 94). Grace herself, in one respect, becomes no more than an investment – 'You'll yield a better return' (*W.* 95) – and her education alongside 'girls... whose parents Giles would have addressed with a deferential Sir or Madam' (*W.* 56) effectively displaces her from the community to which she theoretically belongs: 'She had fallen from the good old Hintock ways'; 'she had latterly become well-nigh an alien [in] her old home' (*W.* 57, 60). Marty South is also the daughter of a (dying) life-holder – 'the social position of the household in the past... definitively shown' by the presence of an old coffin stool, since 'every well-to-do villager, whose tenure was by copy of court-roll', had always owned one (*W.* 29). However, the Souths are impoverished; and, as the novel opens, the naturally refined Marty, unused to the work, is cutting spars 'at eighteenpence a thousand' (*W.* 30; she can make 2*s.* 3*d.* for a day and half a night's work). But do not let us miss Hardy's passing comment that there is nothing in the 'fundamental shape' of 'so many right hands born to manual labour' to confirm the 'conventional' view that 'gradations of birth show themselves primarily in the form of this member', adding that 'nothing but a cast of the die of destiny' has meant that the fingers grasping the bill-hook 'might have skilfully guided the pencil or swept the string, had they only been set to do it in good time' (*W.* 30). 'Character' does not appear to be 'Destiny' here; rather, the effects of a social satire implied by the cast of the dice of 'gradations of birth'. Felice Charmond is the young widow of a 'rich man engaged in the iron trade in the north' (*W.* 209) whose fortune had bought Hintock House and the surrounding woodlands (compare Paula Power and Alec d'Urberville); but her mother had known that 'my face was my only fortune' (*W.* 177), and Felice had been 'a play-actress for a short while' before Mr Charmond married her (*W.* 209). Now, however, despite 'her adaptable, wandering, *weltburgerliche* nature' (*W.* 72), she is the landlord of most of the inhabitants of the area. And Fitzpiers, a doctor and 'so modern a man in science and aesthetics' (*W.* 154), with 'his keenly appreciative, modern, unpractical mind' (*W.* 122), is the last scion of an ancient family: 'Mr Fitzpiers's family were lords of the manor for I don't know how many hundred years.... Why, on the mother's side he's connected with the long line of the Lords Baxby of Sherton'; and 'though he belongs to the oldest, ancientist family in the country, he's stooped to make hisself useful like any common man' (*W.* 153, 61). He is 'a somewhat rare kind of gentleman...to have descended, as from the clouds, upon Little Hintock' (*W.* 105), but he too is 'poor' (*W.* 177), and it is easily overlooked that Hardy lets us know it is Mr Melbury's money which would have set up Fitzpiers's medical practice in 'Budmouth' (*W.* 161–2).

The substance of the novel, therefore, is what happens when this unstable mixture of socially volatile elements – or, as the novel pointedly puts it, 'these people with converging destinies' (*W.* 58) – is thrown together. Melbury's elevation of Grace by education means that she, like Clym Yeobright, returns as the (ironic) 'native' to a community in which she no longer belongs and cannot accept Giles as a suitable marriage partner; but neither does she belong to the society which her fellow-pupils at the boarding school inhabit, nor to the sophisticated but parasitic *rentier* ambience of Felice Charmond and Fitzpiers. Giles, of course, is immobilized and finally destroyed by the disintegration of his social and economic *locus*: the demand for his skills is in decline; his business and attitude to it lack the entrepreneurial vigour of Melbury; and he is subject, too, to the depredations of a newer kind of economic organization – that of the capital-backed proprietorship of his alien landlord, Mrs Charmond. When the last life 'drops' on Giles's houses with the death of Marty South's father and reverts to her estate, Felice is deaf to any plea: 'Mrs Charmond sees no reason for disturbing the *natural course* of things, particularly as she contemplates pulling the houses down' (*W.* 109; emphasis added). In an echo of *The Mayor of Casterbridge*, the locals comment: 'Pulling down is always the game' (*W.* 109); and the novel later glosses this 'natural course' of dispossession as 'the landlords' principle at this date of getting rid of cottages wherever possible' (*W.* 174). The irony in the word 'principle' is heavy indeed. Mrs Charmond is no more part of the Hintock community than Eustacia and Wildeve are of Egdon Heath, but she is more disruptive because she also has financial and legal power. That she uses it irresponsibly, however, is less a reflex of her 'character' than of her social dislocation: the poor-genteel society girl become wealthy heiress and 'lady' of a rural community has no relation to it except in terms of ownership and rents. Like Eustacia, she is bored by her location, and any release from her displaced life there is to be pursued: hence her recognition of Fitzpiers as a kindred spirit in sophisticated deracination – their affair, of course, destroying, in all but name, his marriage to Grace. Fitzpiers himself – a compound of what Hardy was later to separate out as Angel and Alec in *Tess* – is indeed sophisticated: a 'modern', abstractly intellectual dilettante. But he is also sexually predatory – the erotically charged scenes with the village girl Suke Damson (who is herself 'metamorphic' – she is described as 'ambitious' (*W.* 298), and finally emigrates to New Zealand with her betrayed husband) pointing to the destructiveness of this loose spirit. Characteristically, it is his (literally worthless) family lineage which is his attraction for Mr Melbury, just as, conversely, his education and sophistication make Grace see him as not a 'native' either, and therefore 'her' kind of person. Both misrecognitions are the result of the ironic confusions set up by a metamorphic society; and my point is that *The Woodlanders* is less concerned with individual tragedies than with the satire of social relations consequent on the conjuncture of its protagonists factitiously ranked by a class system.

To make this point more conclusively, however, demands some account of the formal properties of the fiction which sustain the satire; and, once seen, the evidence is everywhere apparent. Three aspects will suffice here: the ending, the characterization, and, in relation to both of these, the mode of presentation. The resolution of the plot is where we might expect to find a tragic climax, but in various ways the novel refuses our expectations of any conventional form of such. First, what are we to make of the undisguisedly melodramatic demise of Mrs Charmond reported in chapter XLIII? Following a row with Fitzpiers sparked off by his reading aloud, in 'playfully *ironical* tones' and in a manner 'finely *satirical*', a letter from Marty South regarding 'a certain personal adornment common to herself and Mrs Charmond' (i.e. Marty's hair), Felice is shot dead in Germany by 'a disappointed lover' – 'a South Carolina gentleman of very passionate nature' – who afterwards shot himself. 'That was how it had begun', the novel comments, 'and tragedy had been its end' (*W.* 289–90). Is this, in fact, *tragedy* – or self-parodic burlesque? Conversely, Giles, the 'tragic hero' of the novel, simply fades out: he falls ill with a fever ('possibly typhoid' (*W.* 283)) and a little while later 'passed quietly away' (*W.* 284). Following Giles's unheroic death, however, is a series of false endings centring on the farcical process of Fitzpiers's and Grace's reunion. There is, for example, the wildly 'improbable' sequence in chapters XLVI–XLVII whereby Tim Tangs's jealous fear of Fitzpiers and Suke meeting to say farewell on the eve of her sailing to New Zealand leads to his setting a man-trap – which, in the event, springs shut on Grace's skirt; or the 'implausible' business of Melbury coming across Grace and Fitzpiers by chance in an inn – 'that newly-done-up place – the Earl of Wessex' (*W.* 316) – where she tells him inconsequentially that she 'was nearly caught in a man-trap' (*W.* 319). We are left to assume that she accompanies Fitzpiers – her true 'man-trap' – to his new medical practice 'in the Midland counties' (*W.* 320), and with that this 'tragic' story fizzles out too. The novel ends, finally, first with the comic chorus of rustics discussing women and marriage, and then with the moving elegy to Giles delivered by the ethereal Marty South, who nevertheless, even now, is oddly described as having 'rejected with indifference the attribute of sex for the loftier quality of abstract humanism' (*W.* 323). The ending, then, is not one which allows us comfortably to feel that we are in the presence of high tragedy.

Furthermore, our ability to identify with or 'get inside' the main characters is problematized by the way they are presented to us. Giles, for example, never develops beyond the opening description of him as having 'reserve in his glance, and restraint upon his mouth' (*W.* 38), nor as being 'extremely blank at what he had done' (*W.* 67). Indeed, he does almost nothing in the course of the novel – except assist in his own failure and death – and his passivity seems to symbolize the fact that his kind of life is itself passé. Equally, the breakdown in personal relations that Grace experiences in her class displacement seems to produce her trance-like state throughout the novel (Tess is affected similarly at times) and in which – 'character-less', as it were – she merely embodies her own social and sexual construction by others (e.g. 'Fitzpiers acted upon her like a dram, exciting her, throwing her into a novel atmosphere which biassed her doings until the influence was over' (*W.* 151). Indeed, the novel early on gives the clearest possible indication of its attitude to Grace's character, and to the problematics of characterization in general:

> It would have been difficult to describe Grace Melbury with precision, either then or at any time. Nay, from the highest point of view, to precisely describe a human being, the focus of a universe, how impossible! [Remember the 'impossibility' of 'precisely/fitly describing' De Stancy and Paula in the passage from *A Laodicean* analysed above.] But apart from transcendentalism, there never probably lived a person who was in herself more completely a *reductio ad absurdum* of attempts to appraise a woman, *even externally*, by items of face and figure. (*W.* 52–3; final emphasis added)

Grace, as with Hardy's later ironic attempt to 'faithfully present' Tess as '(a) pure woman' (see below), is 'in herself ... a *reductio ad absurdum* [the phrase itself is a pointed one] of attempts to appraise a woman...', and the impossibility (*pace* realism) of rendering Grace's 'character' – except as a reflex of how she is seen by others – is emphasized once more: 'What people therefore saw of her in a cursory view was very little; in truth, mainly something that *was not she*. The woman herself was a *conjectural creature* who had little to do with the outlines presented to Sherton eyes' (*W.* 53; emphases added). So Grace remains a 'conjectural creature', characterized in the novel only by her metamorphic social position. Conversely, the *active* agents of social dislocation, the outsiders Fitzpiers and Mrs Charmond, are presented in stagey and 'externalized' terms – as though the allusion to melodrama and Sensation-writing is a formal strategy to identify them immediately as 'characters' artificially constructed by a meretricious class society. Fitzpiers's early wooing of Grace, for example, is framed thus: 'At moments there was something theatrical in the delivery of Fitzpiers's effusion' (*W.* 129); and the scenes in which he and Felice begin their affair are overtly in the Sensational mode:

> by the light of the shaded lamp he saw a woman of elegant figure reclining upon a couch in such a position as not to disturb a pile of magnificent hair [Marty South's] on the crown of her head. A deep purple dressing-gown formed an admirable foil to the peculiarly rich brown of her hair-plaits; her left arm, which was naked nearly up the shoulder, was thrown upwards, and between the fingers of her right hand she held a cigarette, while she idly breathed from her delicately curled lips a thin stream of smoke towards the ceiling.
>
> Mrs. Charmond did not move more than to raise her eyes to him, and he came and stood by her. She glanced up at his face across her brows and forehead, and then he observed a blush creep slowly over her decidedly handsome cheeks. Her eyes, which had lingered upon him with an inquiring, conscious expression, were hastily withdrawn, and she mechanically applied the cigarette again to her lips. (*W.* 175)

It is no surprise, then, in a text of this kind to find narrative devices and strategies every bit as artificial and self-reflexive as those in satirical comedies like *The Hand of Ethelberta* and *A Laodicean*, nor that they are most apparent in Hardy's representations of the exploitation, reification, and alienation of human relations determined by class and money. Significantly, the wig-maker – in Little Hintock to buy Marty South's hair, and which he merely refers to as 'the article' (*W.* 32) – first sees Marty, as do we, through a brightly-lit window which frames her as object of attention in a way strikingly similar to those used to present Ethelberta as performance and Paula as male fantasy in the passages analysed earlier. Here, the device serves to emphasize Marty's exploitation – cutting spars in a futile attempt to avoid selling her hair to adorn her landlord, Mrs Charmond's head. Commodification could scarcely find a more telling image. But this is not the only example in the novel of such performative metaphoric representation. The strange business of John South's mortal obsession with the elm tree which he fears will fall on his house is directly related to Mrs Charmond's ownership of the tree, of his house when the 'life' falls in, and indeed of Giles's houses which will also be repossessed by her on South's death. Much of the discussion about how to save his life centres on whether the tree can be felled without her permission and whether a tree is worth more than a man's life. In the event, the tree is felled, South dies anyway, and the chain of repossession, dispossession, and demolition of houses gets underway. Significantly, it is Fitzpiers's careless diagnosis which brings this about, and it is also 'a fragment of old John South's brain' – which he must have acquired after the latter's death – that he is 'investigating' (*W.* 130) when Grace first visits him. Even more pointedly, the occasion of that visit, which is the start of Fitzpiers's faithless courtship and marrying of Grace, is her mission on Grammer Oliver's behalf to cancel the bond the latter has made with the doctor, having sold her brain to him on her death for ten pounds. Fitzpiers has literally – but also figuratively – *bought* the old woman's brain. But we should further notice the way Grace's first sight of him, and him of her (Fitzpiers has already glimpsed 'Grace's *exhibition of herself*' framed in a lighted window of her house (*W.* 119; emphasis added), is constructed by the narrative. Fitzpiers is asleep on the couch as she enters his room:

> Approaching the chimney her back was to Fitzpiers, but she could see him in the glass. An indescribable thrill passed through her as she perceived that the eyes of the reflected image were open, gazing wonderingly at her. Under the curious unexpectedness of the sight she became as if spellbound, almost powerless to turn her head and regard the original. However, by an effort she did turn, when there he lay asleep the same as before. (*W.* 125–6).

The sheer artificiality and displacements of the modes of vision, the reification of 'the eyes of the reflected image ... gazing ... at her', the effect on Grace, and the implication of Fitzpiers's deceit, all surely tell us much about the characters here and the nature of the relationship ahead. Indeed, later in the scene – during Fitzpiers's 'theatrical ... effusion' (see above) – Grace wonders if he might have been deceiving her. "Never", said Fitzpiers fervently. "Never could I deceive you"', and the narrative, in an extraordinary and shameless intrusion, comments: 'Foreknowledge to the distance of a year or so in either of them, might have spoilt the effect of *that pretty speech*. Never deceive her! But they knew nothing and *the phrase* had its day' (*W.* 129; emphases added). In fact, within months, having first 'captured' Grace during the Midsummer mating ritual, he opportunistically rolls Suke Damson in the hay the same night.

Finally, in illustrating the non-realist symbolism of the destructive processes of class relations deployed in this anti-pastoral satire, we may return to the motif of the man-trap. The 'improbability' of the business involving one in the final scenes of the novel has been noted above, but the melodramatic treatment of man-traps, and the elaborate and ironic account (in chapter XLVII) of their place in the rural social economy – during those centuries 'which we are accustomed to look back upon as the true and only period of merry England' (*W.* 309) – are heavily underlined metaphors in the narrative as it pursues its burlesque way to the end. They are even more telling if we remember that many pages previously, in chapter VIII, on Grace's first visit to Mrs Charmond, the latter observes – of 'some curious objects against the walls': '"They are man-traps. My husband was *a connoisseur in man-traps* and spring-guns and such articles... He knew the histories of all these – which gin had broken a man's leg, which gun had killed a man.".... She added *playfully*, "Man-traps are of rather *ominous significance* where a person of our sex lives, are they not?"' (*W.* 70; emphases added). Grace replies that they are 'interesting, no doubt, as relics of a barbarous time happily past', and Mrs Charmond, 'with an indolent turn of her head', concludes: 'Well, we must not take them too seriously.' It is emphatically clear, however, that the novel disagrees, taking them *very* seriously – if satirically – as metaphors for the 'ominous' social and sexual 'significance' of irresponsible new money (Mr Charmond, pointedly, had been in 'the iron trade') and of factitious rank: as the man-traps of a new kind of 'barbarism'. And it is at extreme fictional pains to make sure we see the connection.

Tess of the d'Urbervilles – often regarded as the peak of Hardy's tragic fictional achievement (despite being, for many critics, full of his characteristic 'flaws') – is, to my mind, as clearly written from within the same mindset as that governing any of the satirical 'minor novels'. Precision of class location is once again painstakingly exact. Tess herself, of course, is the last flowering of a noble (and predatory) old family which has now declined into being hagglers. But she is both of, and not of, her community: having 'passed the Sixth Standard in the National

School under a London-trained mistress, [she] spoke two languages' – the local dialect and 'ordinary English' (*T.* 41). Hardy reinforces the point two pages later: 'between her mother... and the daughter, with her trained National teachings and Standard knowledge under an infinitely Revised Code, there was a gap of two hundred years... When they were together the Jacobean and the Victorian ages were juxtaposed' (*T.* 43). Although she 'had held a leading place' in the village school, as soon as she left she lent 'a hand at haymaking or harvesting on neighbouring farms; or by preference, at milking or butter-making processes' (*T.* 55). Alec Stoke d'Urberville's father, old Mr Simon Stoke – 'an honest merchant (some said money lender)' – has bought her ancient family name, with wealth made 'in the North', in order to obscure the 'smart tradesman of the past' (*T.* 56). Alec himself, then, is clearly a second-generation *arriviste* 'gentleman'; and his 'almost new' country house, of 'rich red colour' where 'everything looked like money – like the last coin issued from the Mint' (*T.* 55–6), bears this out, together with its intrusiveness: it has been built in the midst of 'a truly venerable tract of forest land, one of the few remaining woodlands in England of undoubted primaeval date' (*T.* 56). Angel Clare, the third son of an evangelical clergyman, is a 'free-thinker' who has decided not to go to Cambridge and take holy orders like his brothers, but to train to become a farmer 'in the Colonies, America, or at home' in order to protect his 'intellectual liberty' (*T.* 129).

What is apparent from this brief account of the novel's main characters is that Hardy seems to be even more emphatically focusing on displaced 'metamorphic' individuals whose interrelationship becomes increasingly destructive. Whilst the degree to which 'The Woman Pays' (the title of Phase the Fifth in *Tess*) in terms of sexual, economic, and intellectual exploitation by her two lovers (representing irresponsible new money and feckless 'modernism') should not be underestimated, the full social tragedy – if that is what it is – actually comprises the intersection of *all three* of the protagonists' lives. Hardy's profoundly alienated class-consciousness perceives individual social interpellation as more complex and determinate than the mechanistic 'victimization' of one individual by society (in the shape of two others who represent patriarchal injustice). Tess,

Alec, and Angel are so formed and positioned by 'circumstance', especially of their transitional class location, that – in proximity to each other, and in an environment, itself in transition, to which none of them quite belongs – they *must* interact in the way they do. Men like Alec and Angel *will* turn women like Tess into fetishised objects (or 'images') of their sexual or idealist fantasies, and women like Tess – between two worlds – *will* be powerless to resist their own reification in those terms: hence the devastating irony of the full subtitle to the novel: *A Pure Woman Faithfully Presented by Thomas Hardy.*[10] The irony here lies not in the ethical question of whether Tess is 'pure' or not (in the 1892 Preface to *Tess*, Hardy significantly attempts to release that word from 'the artificial and derivative meaning which has resulted to it from the ordinances of civilization'), but, first, in whether there can ever be a 'pure woman' – in the ontological or essentialist sense – when individuals exist only as the images constructed by their social others; and, secondly, in whether, then, 'faithful presentation' – by a novelist, or indeed anyone else – is even remotely possible. On the contrary, the irony is that it is the novelist who constructs the images which represent the woman in the discourse of the fiction. In this scenario, the notion of 'character' – the very heart of humanist realism, with its necessarily essentialist premiss of 'pure' being – becomes problematical to the point of negation. So Hardy's satire, I would argue, is not merely directed at the pretensions and illusions of Christian or humanist belief in the sanctity of the human individual in a society which, by its nature, must foreclose on such, but also at a literary genre which claims the realistic portrayal of 'character' as its central concern and achievement.

With such a conception of satire in view, we may begin to reconsider Hardy's fictional strategies in *Tess*, and find that the 'improbabilities' and 'flaws' are, indeed, part of the project. Events of implausible chance, coincidence, and contingency – the death of the Durbeyfields' horse; the letter to Angel under the mat; the removal of Tess's boots from the hedge by Angel's erstwhile Intended, Mercy Chant, 'that nice girl' who comments – with all the 'mercy' in the world – that the boots have been left by 'some imposter who wishes to come into the town barefoot, perhaps, and so excite our sympathies' (*T.* 286) – become metaphoric representations of a social order in which injustice is endemic and determinate, and where Character is by no means Fate. Similarly, scenes of Sensational or melodramatic power (for example, the sleep-walking Angel laying Tess in the stone coffin, or Alec leaping up off the sarcophagus lid) have an overt symbolic function and simultaneously remind us that this is indeed fiction – thus denying the realist illusion of making an 'utterly false' representation of human life appear to be the truth. The characterization of Tess herself is almost invariably done in terms of 'the spectacle' (*T.* 61) she presents to others, and men in particular – for instance: 'She had an attribute which amounted to a disadvantage just now; and it was this that caused Alec d'Urberville's *eyes to rivet themselves upon her.* It was a luxuriance of aspect, a fullness of growth, *which made her appear more of a woman than she really was*' (*T.* 59; emphases added); or, conversely: 'she mercilessly nipped her eyebrows off, and thus insured against aggressive admiration . . . "What a moppet of a maid!" said the next man she met . . . ' (*T.* 269). Such representation surely confirms the 'external' nature of her characterization as noted in relation to Grace Melbury earlier. But Alec especially is inescapably presented in such a way as to challenge the very principles of realist characterization; he is unequivocally the stagey melodrama villain:

> He had an almost swarthy complexion, with full lips, badly moulded, though red and smooth, above which was a well-groomed black moustache with curled points . . . There was a singular force in the gentleman's face, and in his bold rolling eye.
>
> 'Well, my Beauty, what can I do for you?' said he . . . (*T.* 57)

> The driver was a young man of three- or four-and-twenty, with a cigar between his teeth; wearing a dandy cap, drab jacket, breeches of the same hue, white neckcloth, stick-up collar, and brown driving gloves – in short, he was the handsome, horsey young buck who had visited Joan a week or two before . . . (*T.* 67)

Equally 'improbable' is his later conversion to preacher, but both representations, to my mind, are less failures in Hardy's craft than enactments at once of the artificiality of his 'character' and of the way class and gender construct human subjects socially and fictionally. Overlaying all these obtrusively fictive elements in the novel is the continuously knowing, mannered, and ironically detached narrative voice:

> Thus Tess walks on; a figure which is part of the landscape... Inside this *exterior*, over which the eye might have roved as over a thing scarcely percipient, almost inorganic, there was the record of a pulsing life which had learnt too well, for its years, of the dust and ashes of things, of the cruelty of lust and the fragility of love. (*T.* 269; emphasis added)

What the novel knows it is so clearly giving us is that seen 'exterior' (as with Grace Melbury's 'externality'), and absolutely not the 'inside... record of a pulsing life'; for Hardy is not really concerned with Tess's *character*, but rather with the satire of what *happens to her*. It is no accident, I think, that the final paragraph of the novel should begin with the now famous sentence: '"Justice" was done, and the President of the Immortals, in Aeschylean phrase, had ended his sport with Tess' (*T.* 373). We should be alert to two details, however: first, the ironic quotation marks around 'Justice'; and, second, that 'in Aeschylean phrase' refers to 'the President of the Immortals' and *not*, as might be thought, to 'had ended his sport with Tess'. In other words, it is *Hardy* who presents Tess's tragedy as 'sport' (or 'satire') – the very self-consciousness of the phrasing, right at the end, reminding us that that is how we should have read the entire fictive contrivance preceding it.

There is so much to say – indeed has been said – about *Jude the Obscure*, Hardy's last written novel, that the following brief comments will merely point to the way it represents a culmination of the features of Hardy's fiction identified so far. As implied earlier, while it has no 'lady' in it, it seems in several respects to close the circle begun thirty years before with the 'sweeping dramatic satire' and 'socialistic, not to say revolutionary' writing of *The Poor Man and the Lady*. Certainly, *Jude* was a *succès d'exécration* when it was first published – fulfilling Meredith's warnings about Hardy's early novel receiving 'severe strictures', being 'attacked on all sides', and doing the young novelist's career prospects no good at all. There is, therefore, a Hardyan irony in the fact that *Jude*'s reception was a factor in his decision to give up writing fiction: 'the experience completely curing me of further interest in novel-writing' (1912 'Postscript' to the 1895 Preface). Much of the late-Victorian flak was occasioned by the novel's 'morality', especially in relation to the marriage laws, but it is a discomforting book to read in all sorts of ways, and my feeling is that it was the novel's assault on so many cherished tenets of humanism – and on its handmaiden, realism – which provoked the antipathy it inspired.

For a start, it is a 'Wessex novel' only in a pointedly perverse way, since it abjures rural Dorset, the heart of Wessex, by beginning in 'Marygreen' (Fawley, a village in Berkshire, and Jude's surname) and by locating most of its action in the large towns and cities in more peripheral parts of the region – Reading ('Aldbrickham'), Wantage ('Alfredston'), Newbury ('Kennetbridge'), Salisbury ('Melchester'), Oxford ('Christminster'), Bournemouth ('Sandbourne'), Basingstoke ('Stoke-Barehills'), Winchester ('Wintoncester'). Furthermore, even Marygreen is subject to modernization: 'many of the thatched and dormered dwelling houses had been pulled down of late years [as in *The Mayor of Casterbridge* and *The Woodlanders*], and many trees felled on the green', while the ancient church has been 'taken down... and a tall new building of modern Gothic design...erected on a new piece of ground by a certain obliterator of historic records who had run down from London and back in a day' (*J.* 30–1). Even more to the point, the novel's opening line begins: 'The schoolmaster was leaving the village...' (*J.* 28) – a telling indicator of the novel's fundamental *donnée,* for everything here is in transition and everyone in transit. In this connection, we should register the preposition in the title of each of the parts: 'At Marygreen', 'At Christminster', 'At Melchester', 'At Shaston', 'At Aldbrickham and Elsewhere', 'At Christminster Again', with its clear implication of *sojourning* rather than *dwelling,* of the peripatetic lives of the characters: on the move, unsettled – *vagrant* in its primary sense. Indeed, one of the difficulties of comprehending and remembering the novel is our uncertainty as to where the characters and events are located at any given moment – an instance, perhaps, of the novel's performative narrative strategies.

In respect of the main characters, we are left in little doubt as to their 'metamorphic' nature. Phillotson seeks to better himself by becoming 'a university graduate... then to be ordained' by moving to the 'headquarters' of such aspirations in Christminster (*J.* 29). Arabella, the daughter of a pig-breeder, having married and deserted the bookish Jude, emigrates to Australia, marries into the licensing trade (the public house in Lambeth is 'situated in an excellent, densely populated, gin-drinking neighbourhood' (*J.* 211)), works as a barmaid, and, at the end, is being courted by the (quack) physician, Vilbert. Sue is the daughter of an 'ecclesiastical worker in metal' (*J.* 54) who passes the Queen's Scholarship examination to enter a teacher-training college at Melchester in order to become a schoolmistress (see earlier for a comment on this profession for women); she is a religious free-thinker, and is also, the Preface tells us, a 'delineation' of 'the woman who was coming into notice in her thousands every year – the woman of the feminist movement – the slight, pale "bachelor" girl – the intellectualized, emancipated bundle of nerves that modern conditions were producing mainly in cities as yet': that is, the 'New Woman' of the later nineteenth century – itself an indicative label. Finally, there is Jude himself: an orphan originating from 'Mellstock' (Hardy's birthplace), of parents whose class position is for once unspecified, autodidact and stonemason, and who is described as 'a species of Dick Whittington' (*J.* 97) but who signally fails to find the streets of Christminster paved with gold. The rejection letter he receives from Biblioll College contains this (devastating) 'terribly sensible advice': 'you will have a much better chance of success in life by remaining in your own sphere' (*J.* 136–7). But the point surely is that Jude – and all the other burgeoning members of the 'metamorphic classes' – *have* no sphere of their own to remain in: their condition is, precisely, to be in transit – therein lies the satire of their circumstance.

And satire, I want to claim, is what the novel most emphatically is. The Preface may speak of 'the *tragedy* of unfulfilled aims', of '*tragedies* in the forced adaptation of human instincts to rusty and irksome moulds', of the marriage laws as supplying 'the *tragic* machinery of the tale' (emphases added), but the entire textuality of the novel seems designed to undercut any pretence of tragedy. Even at the levels of plot and character, 'tragic' seems an inappropriate word. Jude may have 'noble' aspirations, but these are constantly degraded by Carnival: his recitation of the names of classical writers is punctuated by the pig-girls' 'Ha, ha, ha! Hoity-toity!' (*J.* 57); and his grandiloquent idealistic fantasy of the scholarly life – 'Yes, Christminster shall be my Alma Mater; and I'll be her beloved son, in whom she shall be well pleased' – is shattered by the arrival of the pig's genitals (*J.* 58). It is also striking that the 'theme' of Jude's high ambition is actually over by the end of Part the Second, Chapter VI (i.e. a third of the way through the novel), the rest being largely taken up with his fraught sexual relationships with Sue and Arabella – hardly, then, a 'heroic' story of devoted struggle leading to tragic failure. Nor is Jude notably 'a Man of Character' – except in the sense I suggested Henchard was above; rather, he is a sympathetic man – more than a little *moyen sensuel* – whose susceptibility to women and drink is his direct undoing. What Jude as 'character' *does* do, however, is act as a device for focusing the injustice and inequity of the social institutions which govern his life. Equally, Sue is not built on a tragic scale, but rather, as many recent (feminist and other) critics have pointed out, represents a deadly 'delineation' – whether misogynistic or not – of the 'New Woman': a kind of feminized Angel Clare. But if we turn, finally, to the novel's third protagonist, Arabella – and one to whom most criticism, in its privileging of the 'tragic' Jude/Sue story, has given cursory attention – we find a more dynamic and instrumental figure in the satire. No one claims that Arabella is tragic, her coarse and fleshy sensuality pointing the other way; but we should not fail to recognize that it is her continual reappearances throughout the text which centrally drive the plot along, and also, as we shall see, it is she who concludes it. If Arabella is Nemesis, then Tragedy becomes 'sport' indeed. We will need to give some hard thought to what Arabella may mean in the totality of this novel.

But the satire of *Jude* is as much in the fictional discourses themselves as in its content or themes. I would not be the first to point to the novel's epigraph as an instruction on how to read what follows. 'The letter killeth' (from 2 Cor. 3: 6) is also quoted in the text by Jude (*J.* 407), where it points to the destructiveness of abiding by the 'letter' of social law rather than obeying emotional 'spirit'. But the phrase's very 'literariness' (to do with 'letters') suggests another level of reading – concerned with textuality itself. It may suggest that 'the letter' of a purported, but necessarily always factitious, 'literal truth' 'killeth' by its (ideological) falsification and misrepresentation; but the 'spirit' of a text – which flouts, subverts, and challenges 'lit/letteral' realism – perhaps 'giveth life'. *Jude,* let us remember, is described in the 1895 Preface as giving 'shape and coherence to a series of seemings, or personal impressions, the question of their consistency or their discordance, of their permanence or their transitoriness, being regarded as not of the first moment'.

I would argue that the novel's performative anti-realism is centrally directed at the 'killing' fictions fostered by a Christian class society, a central one of which is the misrepresentation that there can be 'literal truth' – a misrepresentation mirrored by realism in art. After all, Hardy stopped writing fiction after *Jude*: perhaps he had taken it to the point of auto-deconstruction.

A few examples of the novel's self-advertising fictionality will make the point. In terms of the plot, there is the parallel absurdity of the way the main characters remarry each other; the fortuitous 'chance' encounters and re-encounters on which the movement of the novel depends (for example, Arabella's spotting, and then stalking, of Jude and Sue at the Stoke-Barehills agricultural show (Pt V, Ch. 5)); the grotesque melodrama of Little Father Time and the hanged children – 'Done because we are too menny' (*J.* 356). There are the typographical devices in the text: the pointing hand with the inscription 'THITHER J.F.' (*J.* 94); the Greek 'capital *letters*' (emphasis added) spelling 'The New Testament' – 'like the unclosed eyes of a dead man' (*J.* 68 – the 'letter killeth' indeed). There are the many *letters* and notes that pass between characters, again reproduced in the text (e.g. in Part IV, Chapter III), which often have deadly import for their recipients; there are the endless literary references scattered throughout, but most obtrusively so on Jude's first night in Christminster when 'there were poets abroad, of early date and late' (*J.* 99). Quotations from these 'spectres' fill much of the rest of the chapter – spectres to whom, in a revealing passage, 'Jude found himself speaking out loud, holding conversations with them as it were, *like an actor in a melodrama* who apostrophizes the audience on the other side of the footlights; till he suddenly ceased with a start at his *absurdity*' (*J.* 100; emphases added). Whose 'melodrama', we may ask, is 'apostrophizing the audience', whose self-consciousness of 'absurdity' is brought to our attention? It is not without point, either, that the scene is deflated a few lines later by another 'voice [which] reached him out of the shade', that of a policeman – 'a *real* and local voice' (*J.* 100; emphasis added). Stringing all these textual mannerisms together is the insistently ironic, or comically deflationary, narrative voice: the Christminster colleges display 'the rottenness of these historical documents' (*J.* 102); 'Her Majesty's school-inspector', on a 'surprise visit' to Phillotson's school, is described as 'my gentleman, the king of terrors – to pupil-teachers' (*J.* 128); a customer at Arabella's bar is 'a chappie with no chin, and a moustache like a lady's eyebrow' (*J.* 201); there is the absurd fight in Phillotson's schoolroom, which the text itself calls 'a *farcical* yet melancholy event' (emphasis added), and in which, amongst many other comic elements, 'a churchwarden was dealt such a topper with the map of Palestine that his head went right through Samaria' (*J.* 269); Little Father Time is 'Age masquerading as Juvenility, and doing it so badly that his real self showed through crevices' (*J.* 295); and so on.

Once again, however, it is in the ending of the novel that the satire – 'tragedy as farce' – is most marked: in the arch tones of the narrative voice, in the ironic presentation of the events, and in the undisguised artificiality of the scene's enactment. The final chapter opens with an overt narrative intrusion: 'The last pages to which the chronicler of these lives would ask the reader's attention . . .' (*J.* 422); Jude, the 'tragic hero', lies dying; Arabella is 'at the looking-glass curling her hair, which operation she performed by heating an umbrella-stay in the flame of a candle' (*J.* 422), and is waiting to go out and join a 'festivity' in Christminster that day. Leaving Jude sleeping, she departs; Jude awakens, whispers a series of quotations from the Book of Job – four times punctuated typographically by '("Hurrah!")' wafting in on the breeze from the river – and dies. Arabella, invited by some of his workmates to join the festivities, calls in to check on him, discovers he is dead, exclaims, 'in a provoked tone', 'To think he should die just now! Why did he die just now!' (*J.* 425), goes out again and reassures the workmen: 'O yes – sleeping quite sound. He won't wake yet' (*J.* 425). In the mêlée on the riverbank that follows, while observing 'the gorgeous nosegays of feminine beauty' and 'collegians of all sorts . . . watching keenly for "our" boat' the physician Vilbert slips his arm round her waist, whereupon an 'arch expression overspread Arabella's face' (*J.* 425–6). Back home, she has Jude's body laid out; and, with this done, the narrative comments: 'through the partly opened window the joyous throb of a waltz entered from the ball-room at Cardinal [college]' (*J.* 427). The final ending occurs two days later, just before Jude's funeral, and again the scene is framed by sounds coming in through the window – this time from 'the doctors of the *Theatre*, conferring Honorary degrees on the Duke of Hamptonshire and a lot more illustrious gents of that sort' (*J.* 427; emphasis added). Jude the obscure lies in his coffin; Mrs Edlin and Arabella close the novel; and it is Arabella's voice which has the last word.

How is one to read such a scene? Certainly not, I would suggest, as one of involuntary poor taste, and yet any tragic dignity clinging to Jude is ruthlessly stripped away by the surrounding business of the scene. In effect, then, the focus is not on Jude as tragic hero, but on the 'satire' of Oxford – of the meretricious 'Theatre' that 'Christminster' represents – and of a working-man's aspiration to join it. But why is the venal Arabella at once an element of Carnival in this final scene *and* its dominant 'voice'? My answer will implicate in the satire both Jude himself and Christminster. Much earlier in the novel, after Jude's rejection by Biblioll College, the narrative, on its hero's behalf and in a tone unusually sympathetic and unironic, reflects on the two worlds of Christminster:

> He began to see that the town life was a book of humanity infinitely more palpitating, varied, and compendious than the gown life. These struggling men and women before him were *the reality* of Christminster, though they knew little of Christ or Minster. That was one of *the humours of things*. The floating population of students and teachers . . . were not Christminster in a local sense at all . . .
>
> . . . in pursuit of this idea, he went on till he came to a public hall, where a promenade concert was in progress. Jude entered, and found the room full of shop youths and girls, soldiers, apprentices, boys of eleven smoking cigarettes, and light women of the more respectable and amateur class. He had tapped *the real Christminster life*. (*J.* 137–8; emphases added)

The repetition of the notion that 'reality' and the 'real . . . life' of Christminster lies amongst ordinary working people is a significant one; and perhaps it is this – in his last novel, as in his first – which Hardy wishes to affirm. Hence, whilst Jude and

Sue in their idealism, modernism, and abstraction, are part of the absurd and destructive 'Theatre' of ('gown') Christminster, built on bigotry, class privilege, and injustice, Arabella is not: she must be aligned with the 'light women of the more respectable and amateur class' who comprise the 'real... life' of Christminster. That is another of 'the humours of things'. I do not wish to imply that Hardy makes a sentimental 'salt-of-the-earth' affirmation in Arabella; rather, that this fleshy woman of 'rank passions' (*J.* 398) and a survivor's cunning and vitality, this 'complete and substantial female animal – no more, no less' (*J.* 59), is the ultimate satire on the part of the novel: both within it, as the Carnivalizing degrader of Jude's idealism and Sue's asexuality, and *from* within it – as a 'heroine' who mocks the intellectual pretensions of readers obsessed by the humanist–realist 'tragedy' of Jude's and Sue's story. Arabella 'degrades' us too.

In many respects, Hardy's last published novel, *The Well-Beloved*, emphatically confirms what I have been trying to argue throughout this study so far. Space precludes fuller analysis than the few points I offer here, and I would direct the reader to J. Hillis Miller's penetrating introduction to the 'New Wessex' edition of the novel for further, and by no means dissimilar, treatment of it, and which I return to briefly below.

The publication history of the novel is crucial to its significance: first contracted by Tillotsons in 1890, when the latter had suspended the printing of *Tess* for serial publication and needed something in its place, Hardy worked on 'something light'[11] of about 60,000 words in 1891, the year *Tess* was finally published. *The Pursuit of the Well-Beloved* appeared in twelve weekly parts in the *Illustrated London News* from 1 October 1892. No book edition was published at that point, and Hardy turned to the writing and publication of *Jude*. *The Well-Beloved* was finally published in book form in 1897; for this, Hardy heavily revised several of the early chapters and supplied an entirely different conclusion. It was reprinted, unrevised, in this form for the Wessex Edition of 1912 – with the important addition (see below) of the penultimate paragraph of the Preface, which is also redated 'August 1912' rather than the original 'January 1897'. Straddling the production of *Tess* and

Jude – and clearly, therefore, very much part of their informing mindset – the two versions of the 'same' novel, with their different endings, provoke some tantalizing questions for us. *Which* represents Hardy's 'true' intention? Should we somehow try to read both simultaneously?[12] Is the 1897 book edition in fact, then, Hardy's last novel, and not *Jude* as I have implied above?

Briefly, *The Well-Beloved* is the story of Jocelyn Pierston, a sculptor, who finds his 'ideal' in three generations of women of the same family, all called Avice, and falls in love with each of them, although the love is never reciprocated. The novel ends with Jocelyn married to Maria, a woman he does not love, and his idealist dream recognized to be a chimera. There is no need to point out the extreme artificiality of the plot, but it *is* worth noticing, even here, that Hardy is still concerned with the 'metamorphic classes' – the satire remaining social as well as aesthetic. Pierston is the son of 'an inartistic man of trade and commerce', but is himself a 'sculptor of budding fame' (*WB* 30). The Avices, however, are of 'quarrying' freehold-cottager stock, although the third-generation young woman is herself refined, educated, and runs off to marry the son of a 'Jersey gentleman' who teaches French (*WB* 184). But the satire on art (sculpture/fiction) is the principal discourse of the novel, which the penultimate paragraph added to the 1912 Preface draws attention to:

> As for the story itself, it may be worthwhile to remark that, *differing* from all or most others of the series in that the interest aimed at is of an ideal or subjective nature, and *frankly* imaginative, *verisimilitude* in the sequence of events has been subordinated to the said aim. (Emphases added)

If we recall the Preface to *Jude* – and indeed to several others – then the idea of this novel 'differing' from earlier ones in its 'frank' flouting of 'verisimilitude' is sharply ironic. In fact, many of the self-conscious and mannered features of Hardy's writing which we have noted throughout are only a little more 'frankly' apparent here; and, although Hillis Miller rightly suggests that the novel prompts a retroactive rereading of all Hardy's fiction in the light of what it brings 'fully into the open' (see below), various 'Experiments' at different stages of Hardy's career, as I hope to have shown, have signalled as much if we cared to notice them.

By way of conclusion, we may fittingly glance at the two endings of *The Well-Beloved,* where we can observe the burlesque visceral discourses of Hardy's fiction, finally and once more, on display. The 1892 serial version ends with Jocelyn contrasting 'the ancient Marcia's' 'parchment-covered skull' with a photograph of a young Avice. Struck by 'a sudden sense of *the grotesqueness of things*' (emphasis added), he closes the novel with 'an irresistible fit of laughter', so that the novel's final utterances are *sounds,* not words: 'O – no, no! I – I – it is too, too droll – this ending to my would-be romantic history! Ho-ho-ho!'[13] Or should it be 'my [i.e. Hardy's] history of romancing'? The book version ends with a narrated account of Pierston's current (unidealistic) 'business' – which is, pointedly, to shut down 'the old natural fountains' of the town and pipe in clean water, and to acquire some 'old moss-grown, mullioned Elizabethan cottages' in order, please note, to *pull them down* and build 'new ones with hollow walls, and full of ventilators' (*WB* 205–6). The final paragraph records Pierston's reputation among 'gourd-like young art-critics and journalists' (he is already 'the late Mr Pierston' to them) as 'a man not without genius, whose powers were unsufficiently recognized in his lifetime' (*WB* 206). The ironies are strong in this ending as well, for the idealist artist seems to have become no more than one of the destructive modernizing men we have met in several of the earlier novels; and one wonders if that final 'envoi' is also Hardy, the self-reflexive and undeluded fictionist, signing off too. In any event, these two endings remain unresolved – like so much of Hardy's irony; and it may be, as he himself said in the note on the endings of *The Return of the Native,* that it is for the reader to choose 'the true one'. In which case, I will opt without hesitation for: 'Ho-ho-ho!' greeting 'the grotesqueness of things'.

It seems clear to me, however, that the final book version of this strange novel must, indeed, be regarded as Hardy's last statement in full-length fiction – even if its very oddity and lightness make it look like a minor coda following the real finale of *Jude.* As such, it may be regarded as a kind of retrospective gloss on the preceding *œuvre.* Hillis Miller has put it exactly as I would want to:

> In *The Well-Beloved* the somewhat covert structure and meaning of the earlier novels is brought fully into the open. *The Well-Beloved* functions as an interpretation of the earlier novels or even as their parody. By presenting a schematic and 'unrealistic' version of the pattern they all share, it brings out their latent meaning. It calls attention to the geometric artifice of Hardy's stories. This artifice is masked in the earlier novels by the greater psychological and social verisimilitude... of life as it is, or at any rate of life as it was represented by the great Victorian realists.[14]

My notion of the 'pattern' in Hardy's fiction may differ from Hillis Miller's, and I have further wanted to argue that even in the 'major' works the 'masking verisimilitude' of their apparent realism does not occlude their tendency to self-parody, but otherwise his notion of 'covert' and 'latent' structures and meanings and the 'calling to attention' of 'geometric artifice' is most persuasive. Elsewhere in his essay, Miller notes the 'clash of incompatible features, mimetic realism in the mode of representation and fantasy in the action'; that in *The Well-Beloved*'s overt displaying of 'the fictionality of fiction', it challenges the assumptions of Victorian realism and looks towards modernism; that the co-presence of the two 'endings' refuses the conventional notion of a 'definitive meaning' which the 'telos' of the traditional conclusion seems to give and 'reinforces the reader's sense that the novel is contrived, fantastic, openly fictional, detached from any model in the "real world"'. Hardy, he says, in completely revising the ending, affirms 'his sovereign power as creator over a fiction which no longer needs to validate itself by its presumed correspondence to some "reality" outside literature'. Miller also makes the suggestive hint that, having reached such a position, to go on writing 'Victorian' novels 'in the same way' and 'with a clear conscience' is so problematical that 'novel-writing becomes impossible'.[15] Hence, we may infer, the shift to poetry.

5

Hardy the Poet

With the publication of *Jude* and *The Well-Beloved*, then, Hardy gave up writing prose fiction. The reasons for this may be summed up as follows. First, partly financial: when he could afford to stop producing novels, he did so; secondly, partly personal: the scandalized response of the late-Victorian moralizing lobby to *Tess* and *Jude* had seriously depressed him; thirdly, partly aesthetic: as the preceding chapter has sought to show, Hardy's fictional writing was increasingly pressing against the limits of nineteenth-century realist conventions, challenging and subverting them, and he seems to have reached a formal *impasse* in giving expression to his world-view. *The Life*, of course, as we saw earlier, invariably denigrates his novel-writing career and presents him as *always* primarily a poet, so to suggest that he was first a novelist and then a poet is to misrepresent him – at least in his own estimation; and on his shift of genre in the 1890s, it comments that, 'if he wished to retain any shadow of self-respect', he must abandon fiction and 'resume openly that form of [literary art] which had always been instinctive with him ... the change, after all, [being] not so great as it seemed. It was not as if he had been a writer of *novels proper* ...' (*Life*, 291, emphasis added). That final loaded phrase is further amplified by a memorandum of March 1886 reflecting on the future of prose fiction:

> novel-writing cannot go backward. Having reached the analytic stage it must transcend it by going still further in the same direction. Why not by rendering as visible essences, spectres, etc., the abstract thoughts of the analytic school? ... Abstract realisms to be in the form of Spirits, Spectral figures, etc.... The Realities to be the true realities of life, hitherto called abstractions. The old material realities to be placed behind the former as shadowy accessories. (*Life*, 177)

In itself, this is an indicative statement about Hardy's attitude to fiction in the year he published *The Mayor of Casterbridge* and was writing *The Woodlanders* – one which leads him four years later to decide that '"realism" is not Art' (*Life*, 229) – but his retrospective comment on it is even more revealing: 'This notion was approximately carried out, *not in a novel*, but through *the much more appropriate medium of poetry*, in the supernatural framework of *The Dynasts* as also in smaller poems' (*Life*, 177; emphases added). The hundreds of 'smaller poems' were to follow in the succeeding volumes of poetry, but it is not without point that the single major work Hardy undertook after completing the novels was the non-realist epic verse-drama, *The Dynasts*.

Space prevents discussion of this work here, but we may note in passing both that it was long planned – *The Life* characteristically implying, throughout the years dealing with his novel-writing, that it would be Hardy's truly major achievement – and that the first mention of it is in May 1875, when he was engaged in writing his uncompromisingly anti-realist novel, *The Hand of Ethelberta*. If there is any longer any doubt about ironic self-reflexivity in Hardy's work, the reader should turn to the final chapter of that novel, where Ethelberta – financially freed from the need to be a 'professional romancer' – is described as living '"mostly in the library. And, O, what do you think? She is writing an epic poem, and employs Emmeline as her reader"' (*HE* 409). That Hardy's first wife was called Emma is only a secondary cypher here. *The Dynasts* – an enormous poetic drama of the Napoleonic wars never intended for performance in its entirety – combines detailed historical research (and 'real' historical figures) with an ironic cosmology which sees the ruling spiritual presence of the universe as an indifferent 'Immanent Will' and the human beings as essentially will-less: however (self-)important they may be, they are nevertheless depicted as insignificant figures trapped in the toils of Time and Fate. Various choruses of 'Phantom Intelligences' (e.g. the 'Pities' and the 'Spirits Sinister and Ironic') help to articulate this cosmic 'satire', which also involves many modes of writing. Some of these – especially those which ironically intercut disparate short scenes, or the high panoramic 'shots' of large historical events in the wars – have been seen as cinematic in technique (before film was widely developed as an art form), and hence proto-modernist in tendency. The 'much more appropriate medium' of *The Dynasts* thus remains at once a comment on Hardy's uneasy relation to realist fiction and an indication that prose 'Satires of Circumstance' would transmogrify into poetic – if wry and mordant – 'Moments of Vision'.

As observed in Chapter 3, it is the vast bulk of Hardy's shorter poetry which always makes it difficult to deal with, despite the existence now of a tacit critical consensus about the canonic core of his 'finest' poems. My intention here is briefly to try and bring together this familiar Hardy and the less well-known figure represented by some of those poems seldom – if ever – selected, anthologized, or critically acclaimed, and which must, therefore, be among that mass of 'bad', or 'not "good"', poetry we heard the critics identifying earlier. To do this, I will first consider Hardy's perceived achievement as a poet in general – with brief illustrations along the way – then assess what different emphases and inflexions are given to that achievement by returning some of the 'bad' poetry to the recognized *œuvre* – especially that about women and sexuality. Finally, I will compare in a little more detail cognate poems which nevertheless sit markedly on either side of the evaluative line drawn by critical discrimination of the 'true', 'finest', 'great', 'most characteristic' instances of Hardy's poetic work.

If we turn back to T. R. M. Creighton's unintentionally self-parodic statement quoted earlier: that 'my broad classifications – Nature, Love, Memory and Reflection, Dramatic and Personative, and Narrative – can claim almost canonical authority', we may begin to see the shape the familiar canon takes. Four 'classifications' here draw attention to major themes in Hardy's work, and three to important modes of writing in it. To make two large generalizations in reverse order: first, much of the admiration for Hardy's poetry – leaving aside some (mainly earlier) cavils at 'awkwardness', 'clumsiness', 'irregularity', etc. – has increasingly pointed to his range, innovativeness, and technical skill in prosody. Almost every lyric is different in rhythm and rhyme; and rather than any longer being praised as the product of an excellent but 'untrained' ear, they are now recognized to be the result of supreme professional craft. Equally, his style – especially the clotted syntax and eclectic vocabulary – is now seen, not as the flawed 'primitive' poetic discourse of a self-educated rural genius, but as evidence of complex control and dedicated precision in the use of language. Secondly, there is an 'almost canonical' consensus as to what Hardy's 'finest' poems are about. If we add 'Death and the Dead' to Creighton's list, assume that 'Memory' includes Time, and 'Reflection' Hardy's religio-philosophical poetry, then most people would concur that these themes are indeed what we read him for. His most admired poems are those which deal with the sights, sounds, and rhythms of the countryside; with dead lovers, friends, and relatives; with time – especially what Samuel Hynes has called his 'sense of the tragic nature of *all* human existence: the failure of hopes, the inevitability of loss, the destructiveness of time';[1] and with love – pre-eminently in the famous sequence of elegies to his first wife, Emma, 'Poems of 1912–13' in *Satires of Circumstance, Lyrics and Reveries* (1914).

Grouping the poems by theme is, of course, too exclusive and schematic, as Hardy's most characteristic topics interpenetrate widely, but a rough taxonomy would show the following. There are, very obviously, those poems in which he celebrates natural phenomena by way both of sharply precise denotative description and of connotative anthropomorphic empathy: 'An August Midnight' (*PPP*), 'At Day-Close in November' (*SC*), 'At Middle-Field Gate in February' (*MV*), 'Weathers' (*LLE*), 'Snow in the Suburbs' (*HS*), 'Proud Songsters', 'Throwing a Tree' (both *WW*) – with 'Afterwards' (*MV*) as the classic text. Linked, are poems like 'She Hears the Storm' (*TL*), 'A Sheep Fair' and 'Shortening Days at the Homestead' (both *HS*), which combine vivid rural images with a melancholic recognition of time passing and the transitoriness of living things; and related again are those famous poems which descry a rather more metaphysical significance in the counterpoint of natural and human events: 'Neutral Tones', 'Nature's Questioning' (both *WP*), 'The Darkling Thrush', 'In Tenebris I' (both *PPP*), 'The Convergence of the Twain', 'Wessex Heights' (both *SC*), 'In Time of "The Breaking of Nations"' (*MV*). Then there are the lyrically evocative elegies which memorialize the personal and familial past – again, usually involving a celebratory imagery drawn from natural and homely things: 'Thoughts of Phena' (*WP*), 'The Self-Unseeing' (*PPP*), 'The House of Hospitalities', 'Former Beauties', 'A Church

Romance', 'The Roman Road', 'One We Knew' (all *TL*), 'The Oxen', 'Great Things', 'Old Furniture', 'Logs on the Hearth', 'During Wind and Rain' (all *MV*). Most familiar, too, are the many poems which, in diverse ways, deal with ageing, death, and the dead: from the more astringent ones to do with the tensions of becoming old – '"I Look Into My Glass"' (*WP*), 'Shut Out That Moon', 'Reminiscences of a Dancing Man' (both *TL*), 'An Ancient to Ancients' (*LLE*), 'Nobody Comes' (*HS*), 'He Never Expected Much' (*WW*) – through the variously witty or mournful reflections on a beloved's or his own death – 'In Death Divided' (*SC*), 'On a Midsummer Eve', 'Something Tapped', '"Who's in the Next Room?"' (all *MV*), '"I am the One"', 'Lying Awake' (both *WW*) – to those most 'characteristic' poems which, in effect, resurrect the known local dead: 'Friends Beyond' (*WP*), 'Transformations', 'Paying Calls' (both *MV*), 'Voices from Things Growing in a Churchyard' (*LLE*). There are also three smaller categories – although, as we shall see, these become significantly larger when we restore some of the lesser known poetry: first, the poems which centre on female sexuality, often dramatizing the woman's 'voice' – 'She at his Funeral' (*WP*), 'To Lizbie Brown', 'The Ruined Maid' (both *PPP*), 'A Trampwoman's Tragedy' (*TL*), 'The Sunshade' (*MV*); secondly, poems which display humanistic social observation – 'Midnight on the Great Western' (*MV*), 'No Buyers' (*HS*); and, thirdly, Hardy's much anthologized war poems – which again display his de-heroicizing humanism: 'Drummer Hodge' (*PPP*), 'The Man He Killed' (*TL*), 'Channel Firing' (*SC*), 'In Time of "The Breaking of Nations"' (*MV*), 'Christmas: 1924' (*WW*). Finally, there are the poems to and about Emma – all, in one way or another, refashionings of a lost love – which lie at the very heart of Hardy's poetic canon: '"When I Set Out for Lyonnesse"', 'Under the Waterfall' (both *SC*), 'At the Word "Farewell"', 'The Musical Box', 'The Wind's Prophecy' (all *MV*), and, of course, the 'Poems of 1912–13'.

After many years of troubled and soured marital cohabitation, Emma suddenly – and, to Hardy, unexpectedly – died in 1912. Overcome with remorse and guilt, and leaving his new second wife, Florence Emily, at home, the 72-year-old poet revisited the scenes on the North Cornish coast where, forty years before, their intense love affair had blossomed. In a burst of creative energy, he wrote many of the elegies mentioned above, 'rememorying' – to borrow Toni Morrison's word[2] – their romance in 1870 and producing a sequence of poems which seek to revivify the past and erase the stricken years in between. The sense of failure and loss is now charged, paradoxically, with the eroticism which had drained from the relationship itself; and Hardy realizes, in the 'present' of his poetry, the promise of that intense sexual bonding which he and Emma had once experienced and failed to fulfil. Florence Emily Hardy, with an acumen perhaps sharpened by chagrin, is reported as saying: 'all the poems about [Emma] are a fiction but fiction in which their author has now come to believe.'[3] The Emma poems, then, are less ones of nostalgia and regret, and more the reanimation of what Hardy, in his poem 'Thoughts of Phena' (*WP*), called a 'lost prize'. But it is the plangency of the poetic expression in which this fictional 'past' is retrieved that has made these poems so justly admired.

In no way, therefore, is it my intention in the later parts of this study to disavow the quality of the vast majority of the poems mentioned so far, those which comprise the conventional canon of Hardy's 'true' achievement. Many, indeed, are personal favourites – although, like most critics, I find it hard to put my finger on exactly what it is that makes them so. It is, I think, the (apparently) easy control of 'A Darkling Thrush', rather than what it says, which still evokes an awed response from me, as do the upbeat rhythmic drive of 'Reminiscences of a Dancing Man' and the achieved lyric compression of 'Former Beauties'. However familiar, the ponderously ironic language and rhythm of 'The Convergence of the Twain' – '"What does this vaingloriousness down here?"' – retain their defamiliarizing force, just as the painful, slow unfolding of the misery which informs 'Wessex Heights' establishes the experiential authenticity of the poem (see below). In 'Old Furniture', there are the delicately rendered fading images of the past, but it is the characteristic 'turn' at the opening of the final stanza – 'Well, well. It is best to be up and doing' – which refuses the settling comfort of nostalgia in both poem and reader. Whether 'During Wind and Rain' is one of the 'best poems of the century', as some critics contend,[4] is not something I can judge, but there are surely few readers who do not respond to the biting pathos of its ballad-like refrain and its final images: 'Ah, no; the years O! | How the sick leaves reel down in throngs!', nor to the mordant irony of the repetition of 'Gentlemen' in the Yeats-like wittiness of 'An Ancient to Ancients' – especially in the deeply ambiguous compression of its last lines: 'Nay, rush not: time serves: we are going, | Gentlemen'. And the two late poems in *Winter Words*, '"We Are Getting to the End"' and 'He Resolves to Say No More', confirm for me, not only that they are highly achieved and moving 'envoi' lyrics, but that they are so because they deploy so many of the features of Hardy's poetic discourse: the epic scale in the lyric mode; the tightly controlled metre and rhyme-scheme; the occasional unexpected word ('warely', 'charnel-eyed'); the relentless irony ('We ply spasmodically our pleasuring'; 'Magians who drive the midnight quill | With brain aglow | Can see it so'); the tough endings which admit no false illusions. All of which culminates in the satisfying ambivalence of the final stanza of Hardy's 'last' poem ('He Resolves to Say No More' (*WW*)):

> And if my vision range beyond
> The blinkered sight of souls in bond,
> – By truth made free –
> I'll let all be,
> And show to no man what I see.

Nevertheless, the canonic Hardy does seem to stereotype him, and it certainly leaves a lot of poems out – an effect strikingly analogous to that in respect of his 'minor novels'. Characteristically, Hardy the Poet becomes the very English celebrant of Nature and of a passing rural life; the poet who expresses deep personal loss and regret for the pastness of the past, and meditates calmly on Death; a poet also of astringent melancholy at the 'ironies' and 'satires' of human life and aspiration; and one of profound pessimism, tinged with a modicum of redemptive humanism, in the 'Dark Age'[5] of the modern world. It is this 'Georgian' Hardy, leavened with some of the 'gloomy' philosophical poetry and with the elegies to Emma, which represents his quintessential figuration in literary history. But it is *this* Hardy, too, which was recuperated by Donald Davie (see above, Chapter 3), as the anti-'totalitarian' source of a counter-tradition in modern British poetry: a poetry of 'engaging modesty and decent liberalism', which allows the 'slimmest margin' for humanism; of 'extremely limited objectives'; of ironic quietism and personal 'integrity';[6] and whose poetic descendant was Philip Larkin. Words like 'passivity', 'nostalgia', 'pessimism', 'determinism', 'guilt', 'remorse', 'resignation', haunt around this Hardy, who then becomes the ironic apologist for the cultural values of disdainful retreat in the political and intellectual gridlock of postmodern perplexity: apathy, disenchantment, and rural nostalgia in the 'madness' of late-twentieth-century life. Davie may have been right – perhaps this *is* Hardy's defining cultural locus; but it still seems to me to predetermine and constrict our reading of his poetry.

The question will be asked: what, then, changes in our perception of Hardy the poet if we restore to his *œuvre* poems which by and large fall outside the recognized corpus? Well, not a lot in many respects: it is more a matter of small shifts in emphasis than radical difference. An even more extensive inventiveness and diversity in prosody evidences itself; and we may indeed wonder why the metrical skill of comprehensively ignored poems is so little admired: for example, the assured handling of the 'triolet' form in 'The Coquette, and After' (*PPP*; see below), the long idiomatically rhythmical lines of the dramatic monologue, 'The Chapel-Organist' (*LLE*); the lilting song-like measure of the touching lyric 'Queen Caroline to her Guests' (*HS*). Equally, while the *kinds* of poems – their subjects, themes, and tones – may appear similar, it is the range and variety of their treatment which is greatly extended. This is especially true of Hardy's humanistic poems of social observation; but also of that much enlarged group which are concerned with women and sexual relations and in which, beyond the defining frame of the love poems to Emma, he writes obsessively and contradictorily about women of all classes, types, and degrees of familiarity. Overall, *this* Hardy is wittier, more humorous, satirical, and astringent than is normally perceived in the familiar melancholic or nostalgic quietist; more socially engaged and humanistic than the 'pessimistic' determinist; more erotic and libertarian, more contradictorily positioned – as we would expect of the erstwhile novelist – in relation to female sexuality and male attitudes to it than the fixated, chaste, and remorseful lover of 'Poems of 1912–13' might suggest.

A synoptic overview of a few of Hardy's least well-known poems will help to make the point for me. The poem 'Tragedian to Tragedienne' (*HS*), for example, despite its dramatic voice, is as personal and realized a lyric about death, love, and the death of love as many of Hardy's famous poems – as, indeed, is its companion-piece (this time in the woman's voice), 'Circus-Rider to Ringmaster' (*HS*), with its moving final stanza:

> Though not as now when you freshly knew me,
> But a fading form,
> Shape the kiss you'd briskly blow up to me
> While our love was warm.
> And my cheek unstained by tears,
> As in these last years!

The late 'Unkept Good Fridays' (*WW*) is a measured and telling affirmation of ordinary human courage and sacrifice which contrasts well with the 'canonic' pessimism, say, of the early 'To an Unborn Pauper Child' (*PPP*), just as the widely ignored elegy (not, however, to Emma) '"Nothing Matters Much"' (*HS*) – with its subtle revision of the first and last lines and its haunting fourth stanza – is surely comparable with the tough, uncompromising late poems in *Winter Words*. The neat philosophical lyric 'Going and Staying' (*LLE*) is no less memorable than the clearly cognate poem '"We Are Getting to the End"', nor is the seldom-anthologized 'In a Former Resort after Many Years' (*HS*) than its well-known parallel, 'Former Beauties' – although it is doubtless significant that where the latter nostalgically evokes a past(oral) idyll, the other poem forces upon us a grim present reality. Why, one may ask, is the humanistically affirmative 'The Old Workman' (*LLE*) so little known compared, for example, to the less sanguine 'No Buyers'; why has the bitter anti-war sonnet '"Often When Warring"' (*MV*) – again expressing a mundane humanism – fared so badly compared to the similarly themed 'The Man He Killed' or the elegiac 'Drummer Hodge'? Perhaps less puzzlingly unfamiliar are the neurotically sexual 'The Woman I Met', which at once gives a voice to the prostitute and 'speaks' the male's repressed desire; the strange dramatic monologue "The Collector Cleans his Picture', with its overt deconstruction of the masturbatory male gaze; or 'The Chapel-Organist' (all *LLE*), which positively counterposes the woman's voluptuous sexuality and large spirit with the mean prurience of the religious culture she is destroyed by. Such poems clearly do not sit easily next to the 'characteristic' elegiac love poems, to the nostalgic celebratory lyrics like 'To Lizbie Browne', nor even to the wry inverted pastoral of 'The Ruined Maid'. Indeed, what they *do* do, in this unfamiliar juxtapositioning, is to set those poems in a rather more complex sexual frame. For example, the fact that the *positive* female eroticism of a number of other poems, often in the woman's voice (e.g. 'The Dark-Eyed Gentleman', 'One Ralph Blossom Soliloquizes', 'Julie-Jane' (all *TL*), 'In the Days of Crinoline' (*SC*)), is offset by the counter-discourse of female folly and sexual tragedy observed and satirized by male judgement (e.g. in 'On the Portrait of a Woman about to be Hanged' (*HS*) and 'The Elopement' (*SC*), compounds this complexity. Furthermore, it is noteworthy – and perhaps suggestive – how their reinstatement in the canon re-imbeds the other, now critically sanitized, love poetry in the historicized sexual matrix which we have seen shaped Hardy as novelist: at once acutely sensitive to women's lot in late-nineteenth-century society but also contradictorily imbricated, personally and professionally, by patriarchal ideology.

This is not to read Hardy against the grain – the *grain* is very evident beneath the polish and varnish of use and age – but to read against the critical *graining* of his poetry. To take a specific example: in a number of the less well-known poems, it is the woman whose 'voice' the poem articulates – a trope, with minimal exception, that does not feature in the canonic Hardy. These voices express either a robust sexuality and strength – note, for example, the climatic voice of 'Anne' at the end of 'One Ralph Blossom Soliloquizes'(*TL*):

> And Anne cries: 'O the time was fair,
> So wherefore should you burn down there?
> There is a deed under the sun, my Love,
> And that was ours. What's done is done, my Love.
> These trumpets here in Heaven are dumb to me
> With you away. Dear, come, O come to me!'

– or the Tess-like resignation of the second triolet in 'The Coquette, and After' (*PPP*; note 1.3, especially in relation to my earlier discussion of Hardy's views about tragedy):

At last one pays the penalty –
The woman – women always do.
My farce, I found, was tragedy
At last! – One pays the penalty
With interest when one, fancy-free,
Learns love, learns shame.... Of sinners two
At last *one* pays the penalty –
The woman – women always do!

Since 'In a Eweleaze Near Weatherbury' (*WP*) has recently become critically admired and has been misread,[7] we may further note that the voice here – if we are to make sense of the poem, but contrary to first appearances – is also that of the woman. Probably occasioned by the death in 1890 (it is dated '1890') of Hardy's cousin, Tryphena Sparks, with whom he is usually believed to have had a youthful love affair and who had also served a 'term as teacher' (l. 5), the poem seems to represent her voice and not the poet's:

The years have gathered grayly
  Since I danced upon this leaze
With one who kindled gaily
  Love's fitful ecstasies!
But despite the term as teacher,
  I remain what I was then
In each essential feature
  Of the fantasies of men.

Yet I note the little chisel
  Of never-napping Time
Defacing wan and grizzel
  The blazon of my prime.
When at night he thinks me sleeping
  I feel him boring sly
Within my bones, and heaping
  Quaintest pains for by-and-by.

Still, I'd go the world with Beauty,
  I would laugh with her and sing,
I would shun divinest duty
  To resume her worshipping.
But she'd scorn my brave endeavour,
  She would not balm the breeze
By murmuring 'Thine for ever!'
  As she did upon this leaze.

1890

Line 8 – 'Of the fantasies of men' – makes sense only if the speaker is female (a manuscript cancellation – 'And in fervours hid from men' – makes this even clearer); and it is important to recognize that 'he' in l. 13 is 'Time' not the lover, and that 'her' and 'she' in stanza three must be 'Beauty' (l. 17; *not* a female lover) who is 'worshipped' (l. 20) by the female speaker. It is *her* courageous affirmation of 'Beauty', then, and *her* acceptance of its curtailment which the final stanza expresses.

In almost all cases, the woman's voice speaks an honesty and an openness to life and sexuality which the male poems (despite the 'throbbings of noontide' in '"I Look Into My Glass"') seldom have. On the contrary, the latter tend to give utterance to the 'faintheart' who bemoans his 'lost prizes'.[8] Apropos, there has been considerable critical speculation about whether Hardy redeems Emma's 'voice', or silences it, in 'Poems of 1912–13'. But the pervasive elegiac voice of those poems is surely that of Hardy forging a new reality out of a lost, fading, and unfulfilled past. The kind of female voice which speaks in the less familiar poems glanced at above – positively erotic, disruptively strong, and sharply aware of the social victimization of women within patriarchy – could have no place there: Emma must remain the dim voice of 'the woman calling' ('The Voice'), the 'voiceless ghost' ('After a Journey'), in the context of Hardy's poetic remorse and guilt for the lost relationship. The 'woman's voice', here, would have destabilized love poems which so movingly express his attempt to retrieve buried experience – their final balance and equipoise achieved by its exclusion. But those released voices in the less familiar poems insistently press us, now, to wonder what that silenced woman's voice might have said.

Finally, let me place in counterpoint six poems in three pairs – in each case, comprising one canonic poem and one of the least reprinted or critically considered. This is in no sense to diminish the value of the famous one; rather, to attempt to release more of Hardy's work into view and implicitly to uncover the kinds of determining – but usually tacit – premisses on which the valued poetry is based. '"I Found Her Out There"' (*SC*) is one of the most revered lyrical elegies to the young Emma in 'Poems of 1912–13':

I found her out there
On a slope few see,
That falls westwardly
To the salt-edged air,
Where the ocean breaks
On the purple strand,
And the hurricane shakes
The solid land.

I brought her here,
And have laid her to rest
In a noiseless nest
No sea beats near.
She will never be stirred
In her loamy cell
By the waves long heard
And loved so well.

So she does not sleep
By those haunted heights
The Atlantic smites
And the blind gales sweep,
Whence she often would gaze
At Dundagel's famed head,
While the dipping blaze
Dyed her face fire-red;

And would sigh at the tale
Of sunk Lyonnesse,
As a wind-tugged tress
Flapped her cheek like a flail;
Or listen at whiles
With a thought-bound brow
To the murmuring miles
She is far from now.

Yet her shade, maybe,
Will creep underground
Till it catch the sound
Of that western sea
As it swells and sobs
Where she once domiciled,
And joy in its throbs
With the heart of a child.

If we set next to it the comprehensively ignored poem 'Concerning Agnes' (*WW*), we find another elegy – not this time, however, to Emma, but to Lady Agnes Grove, one of the women Hardy fell in love with in the 1890s and who died in 1926:

> I am stopped from hoping what I have hoped before –
> Yes, many a time! –
> To dance with that fair woman yet once more
> As in the prime
> Of August, when the wide-faced moon looked through
> The boughs at the faery lamps of the Larmer Avenue.
>
> I could not, though I should wish, have over again
> That old romance,
> And sit apart in the shade as we sat then
> After the dance
> The while I held her hand, and, to the booms
> Of contrabassos, feet still pulsed from the distant rooms.
>
> I could not. And you do not ask me why.
> Hence you infer
> That what may chance to the fairest under the sky
> Has chanced to her.
> Yes. She lies white, straight, features marble-keen,
> Unapproachable, mute, in a nook I have never seen.
>
> There she may rest like some vague goddess, shaped
> As out of snow;
> Say Aphrodite sleeping; or bedraped
> Like Kalupso;
> Or Amphitrite stretched on the Mid-sea swell,
> Or one of the Nine grown stiff from thought. I cannot tell!

Here again is a celebration of an 'old romance' (l. 8); the direct, personal, and conversational opening; the sense of the frailty of human life and beauty in the relentless process of time ('what may chance to the fairest under the sky | Has chanced to her' (ll. 15–16); and a similar invocation of the endless swell of the oceans. Both poems contain movingly precise images of the 'unapproachable' dead ('Concerning Agnes', l. 18) in their 'nest', 'cell' ('"I Found Her"', ll. 11, 14) and 'nook' ('Concerning Agnes', l. 18); but in 'Concerning Agnes' there is also the finely controlled classical paean of the last stanza, abruptly humanized by Hardy's final admission: 'I cannot tell!' As a hypothetical exercise in the manner of the old 'Practical Criticism', let us try to envisage these two poems as entirely unfamiliar 'unseen' texts (with the identity, of course, of the woman in each unknown), and consider on what critical criteria of poetic excellence we would judge one to be included in a selection of 'great' poems. We would not be able to say that the obscurity of 'the Larmer Avenue' (a public pleasure ground at an estate on the Wiltshire/Dorset border with a large dancing area) in l. 6 of 'Concerning Agnes' is a problem not present in '"I Found Her Out There"', because both 'Dundagel' (l. 22; Tintagel) and 'Lyonnesse' (l. 18; a mythical name for Cornwall) are equally obscure; nor that a word like 'bedraped' ('Concerning Agnes', l. 21) is awkward and strange when we have 'at whiles' and 'domiciled' at ll. 29 and 38 of the other poem; nor that 'the booms | Of contrabassos' ('Concerning Agnes', l. 12) is any more of a hindrance to understanding than 'the purple shroud' (l. 6) or 'her loamy cell' (l. 14) of '"I Found Her Out There"'; nor that the flatly prosaic language and rhythm of 'Concerning Agnes', ll. 5–6 or 13–14, are a blemish, if we cannot convincingly make a case for ll. 9–10 or 21–2 of the other poem. What *intrinsic* quality does criticism descry, then, which makes one of these poems so widely agreed to be among Hardy's 'finest' and the other manifestly not?

A second pair of poems which will bear some comparison are 'Wessex Heights' (*SC*) – to me, as I have indicated earlier, one of Hardy's most impressive achievements – and 'By Henstridge Cross at the Year's End' (*LLE* which is rarely reprinted and scarcely ever mentioned even among the wide diversity of poems Hardy's critics consider).

Wessex Heights
(1896)

There are some heights in Wessex, shaped as if by a kindly hand
For thinking, dreaming, dying on, and at crises when I stand,
Say, on Ingpen Beacon eastward, or on Wylls-Neck westwardly,
I seem where I was before my birth, and death may be.

In the lowlands I have no comrade, not even the lone man's friend –
Her who suffereth long and is kind; accepts what he is too weak to mend:
Down there they are dubious and askance; there nobody thinks as I,
But mind-chains do not clank where one's next neighbour is the sky.
In the towns I am tracked by phantoms having weird detective ways –

Shadows of beings who fellowed with myself of earlier days:
They hang about at places, and say harsh heavy things –
Men with a wintry sneer, and women with tart disparagings.

Down there I seem to be false to myself, my simple self that was,
And is not now, and I see him watching, wondering what crass cause
Can have merged him into such a strange continuator as this,
Who yet has something in common with himself, my chrysalis.

I cannot go to the great grey Plain; there's a figure against the moon,
Nobody see it but I, and it makes my breast beat out of tune;
I cannot go to the tall-spired town, being barred by the forms now
passed
For everybody but me, in whose long vision they stand there fast.

There's a ghost at Yell'ham Bottom chiding loud at the fall of the night,
There's a ghost in Froom-side Vale, thin-lipped and vague, in a shroud
of white,
There's one in the railway train whenever I do not want it near,
I see its profile against the pane, saying what I would not hear.

As for one rare fair woman, I am now but a thought of hers,
I enter her mind and another thought succeeds me that she prefers;
Yet my love for her in its fulness she herself even did not know;
Well, time cures hearts of tenderness, and now I can let her go.

So I am found on Ingpen Beacon, or on Wylls-Neck to the west,
Or else on homely Bulbarrow, or little Pilsdon Crest,
Where men have never cared to haunt, nor women have walked with
me,
And ghosts then keep their distance; and I know some liberty.

By Henstridge Cross at the Year's End

(From this centuries-old cross-road the highway leads east to London, north to Bristol and Bath, west to Exeter and the Land's End, and south to the Channel coast.)

Why go the east road now?...
That way a youth went on a morrow
After mirth, and he brought back sorrow
Painted upon his brow:
Why go the east road now?

Why go the north road now?
Torn, leaf-strewn, as if scoured by foemen,
Once edging fiefs of my forefolk yeomen,
Fallows fat to the plough:
Why go the north road now?

Why go the west road now?
Thence to us came she, bosom-burning,
Welcome with joyousness returning....
She sleeps under the bough:
Why go the west road now?

Why go the south road now?
That way marched they some are forgetting,
Stark to the moon left, past regretting
Loves who have falsed their vow....
Why go the south road now?

Why go any road now?
White stands the handpost for brisk onbearers,
'Halt!' is the word for wan-cheeked farers
Musing on Whither, and How....
Why go any road now?

'Yea: we want new feet now,'
Answer the stones. 'Want chit-chat, laughter:
Plenty of such to go hereafter
By our tracks, we trow!
We are for new feet now.'

During the War

Both poems are deeply personal meditations at times of crisis in the poet's life (the mid-1890s/'During the War'); both use a geographical mapping device to structure the poem (the four 'heights', plus the 'lowlands', in 'Wessex Heights'/ the four 'roads' in 'By Henstridge Cross'); both are complex and knotty in syntax and movement as the poet struggles to give shape to tortuous significances in the tensions of a personal/public history; both, in different ways, master their informing traumas in the tight control of their versification; both, despite the misery which prompts them, end on a note of hard-won affirmation ('I know some liberty'/'"We are for new feet now"'); both are initially, if not ultimately, obscure at times – especially in terms of their biographical reference ('Wessex Heights', in particular, has been subject to extensive – and unresolved, not to say comic – speculation about the identities of the women referred to in it). And yet, despite all this, 'Wessex Heights' is undeniably at the centre of the Hardy canon and 'By Henstridge Cross' is comprehensively ignored. To my mind, the latter's synoptic charting of formative failure and loss in Hardy's life is equally as resonant as the defiant introversion of 'Wessex Heights': stanza one – whatever it was that happened to him in London in the 1860s; stanza two – the decline of his family's fortunes; stanza three – Emma, then wonderfully 'bosom-burning', now dead; and stanza four – culminating in the vast tragedy of the First World War. Furthermore, the fifth stanza – which so characteristically 'turns' the poem towards its conclusion – encapsulates with astonishing economy the poem's telling double perspective: the recognition at once of an irresistible dynamic futurity ('brisk onbearers') and of equally insistent doubts about the point of participating in it. Unexpectedly, and against the grain, the language, rhythm, and sense of this last liberating stanza all affirm the precedence of the former. Perhaps it is this final implicit destabilizing of the 'characteristic' 'gloomy' Hardy which keeps a poem, otherwise pressing for an explanation of its neglect, in non-canonic obscurity.

Let us turn, similarly and finally, to 'The Darkling Thrush' (*PPP*), one of – perhaps *the* – most famous of Hardy's poems.

I leant upon a coppice gate
  When Frost was spectre-gray,
And Winter's dregs made desolate
  The weakening eye of day.
The tangled bine-stems scored the sky
  Like strings of broken lyres,
And all mankind that haunted nigh
  Had sought their household fires.

The land's sharp features seemed to be
  The Century's corpse outleant,
His crypt the cloudy canopy,
  The wind his death-lament.
The ancient pulse of germ and birth
  Was shrunken hard and dry,
And every spirit upon earth
  Seemed fervourless as I.

At once a voice arose among
  The bleak twigs overhead
In a full-hearted evensong
  Of joy illimited;
An aged thrush, frail, gaunt, and small,
  In blast-bruffled plume,

Had chosen thus to fling his soul
  Upon the glowing gloom.

So little cause for carolings
  Of such ecstatic sound
Was written on terrestrial things
  Afar and nigh around,
That I could think there trembled through
  His happy good-night air
Some blessed Hope, whereof he knew
  And I was unaware.

31 December 1900

Let us compare this well-known poem with the once more widely neglected 'On Stinsford Hill at Midnight' (*LLE*); (other lesser-known poems which bear close comparison with 'The Darkling Thrush' are 'The Last Chrysanthemum' (*PPP*) and 'Christmastide' (*WW*)).

I glimpsed a woman's muslined form
  Sing-songing airily
Against the moon; and still she sang,
  And took no heed of me.

Another trice, and I beheld
  What first I had not scanned,
That now and then she tapped and shook
  A timbrel in her hand.

So late the hour, so white her drape,
  So strange the look it lent
To that blank hill, I could not guess
  What phantastry it meant.

Then burst I forth: 'Why such from you?
  Are you so happy now?'
Her voice swam on; nor did she show
  Thought of me anyhow.

I called again: 'Come nearer; much
  That kind of note I need!'
The song kept softening, loudening on,
  In placid calm unheed.

'What home is yours now?' then I said;
  'You seem to have no care.'
But the wild wavering tune went forth
  As if I had not been there.

'This world is dark, and where you are.'
  I said, 'I cannot be!'
But still the happy one sang on,
  And had no heed of me.

Rhythmically not dissimilar to 'The Darkling Thrush', this mysterious poem makes an almost identical statement to it: the 'heedless' happiness of the song of the thrush/woman suggesting some 'blessed Hope' in this 'dark world' which the 'I' of the two poems cannot share. Both poems, it should be noted, remain ambiguous – neither clarifies whether it endorses hope or despondency as the proven reality. While 'On Stinsford Hill at Midnight' clearly does not have the evocative natural description of the opening stanzas of 'The Darkling Thrush' – which certainly may devalue it for inclusion in the 'characteristic' Hardy – it does, nevertheless, have the mystery of its event lyrically defined by the first three eery stanzas, redolent as they are of Hardy's much-praised expropriations from the ballad tradition. Two factors suggest themselves as to why, once again, we may find ourselves puzzled and unconvinced by the consensual elevation of one poem and the relegation of the other: *'on what grounds?'* must be the insistent question. First, Hardy's explanatory subscript note under 'The Darkling Thrush' extra-textually gives that poem much of its reverberating resonance. Without it, 'The Century's corpse outleant' would be even more obscure than it already is, and the whole poem could, only with great effort, be read as a meditation on the turn of the nineteenth century. Secondly, I would repeat that the characteristic – that is, 'great' – Hardy seems to need a voice from Nature (the thrush) and not that of a human being (however ghostly). In effect, the 'heedless' happiness of nature, in its entire alterity from the human, cannot threaten or challenge the validity of the pessimism of the human mind: it is, simply and ironically, *other*. This, then, legitimizes the continued acceptance of despair as a reasonable – perhaps even exemplary – intellectual position. If, on the other hand, the agent of an alternative 'happiness' or 'hopefulness' is human, then that absolute otherness breaks down, pessimism becomes only one intellectual option amongst others, and can be challenged for its egocentricity and passivity. In other words, it can be shown to be able to be overthrown and transcended by the (opposite) human capacity which embraces happiness, hope, futurity, self-determination – everything, in short, that an ideology of quietistic cultural despair rejects. The canonic Hardy, I am arguing by way of 'The Darkling Thrush', tends to underwrite this critical and ideological stance (see Donald Davie above, amongst others rather less explicit), while the neglected poems, at least marginally, problematize it.

My general point, then, is that juxtaposing one kind of poem with another helps to deconstruct the tacit underlying cultural/ideological assumptions and attitudes the 'characteristic' Hardy embodies. It does this, principally and throughout, by the release of sexual affirmation in the woman's voice in many poems, by the refusal to accept despair in others, by the substitution of human agency for Nature's 'heedlessness' in others again, and by thus bringing into view the heterogeneity of a body of poetry which is, indeed, an index of Hardy's struggle to affirm the human capacity for, and will towards, a better life even in a 'new Dark Age'.

6

Conclusion

I began this study by asking in what ways Hardy might be 'our contemporary': widely read, studied, and reproduced, what does his work mean to us in the early twenty-first century? The study's answers, such as they are, have been oblique and implicit, and so perhaps they should be summarized here. First, there is no *one* 'Hardy' – no 'true' or essential figuration to be discovered and revealed amongst all the (mis)representations of him. Leaving aside the more obvious generic distinctions – Hardy the novelist, Hardy the poet (plus Hardy the short-story-writer and essayist: but surely it is indeed a misrepresentation to divide him thus, rather than to see him comprised of all these genres) – we may still see quite different Hardys in the contemporary critical treatment of him as novelist and as poet. In the former case, most modern criticism now evinces the influence of Marxist, feminist, and poststructuralist theories and practices, and Hardy's novels have been refashioned as potentially radical and subversive textualities – a process with which the present study aligns itself. Hardy the poet, on the other hand, remains largely constrained within the naturalized critical consensus both as to his canon of 'finest' work and, co-determinately, to his 'characteristic' nature and achievement. In this case, therefore, I have attempted to bring into view the subliminal construction of Hardy the Poet, and to hint that it might be at once limiting and susceptible to *re*construction. Secondly, and as a consequence of there being no one 'Hardy', it is apparent that there are indeed radically different versions of him simultaneously present in our culture – including, importantly, those implied by the (re)presentations of his texts flickering in increasing numbers across our screens ('1996 . . . the year of the Wessex poet and novelist') whatever it may be we think they imply – if we *do* think about it, that is. Thirdly, following from all this – but also its primary instigation – is the study's belief that, if Hardy *is* our contemporary – as he clearly seems to be – *then it is we who make him so*. His texts are determinate in so far as they physically exist in a more or less established and agreed form (although his *œuvre*, as we have seen, is still subject to manhandling and manipulation), but it is we who 'see in'/'read into' them the Hardy we need – be it the Heritage Hardy or the Deconstructionist *avant la lettre*. *Which* Hardy we want to have as our contemporary is a heavy responsibility for reader and critic – not least in the awesome recognition that reading and criticism in effect construct their own object of attention. Perhaps the undertaker's cat who stole Hardy's heart as it waited for burial in Stinsford churchyard was itself an anti-essentialist contemporary critic *avant la lettre*? Perhaps Hardy willed it to happen? Perhaps the undertaker made the story up? Who knows? But the moral is clear: Hardy's literary body exists as the *corpus* of texts; it is we as critical readers who constantly restore to them a heart which ensures they are alive and kicking in the present.

7

Postscript: Hardy from Page to Screen

A passing remark in the 1996 Conclusion to the first edition of this book noted 'those . . . (re)presentations of [Hardy's] texts flickering in increasing numbers across our screens'. And it is fair to say, as for so many 'classic' authors these days, that a Hardy novice may well first come across his work as a cinema or TV film, since there is now a proliferation of versions of his fiction in this medium.[1] Excellent, of course, if this experience persuades the novice to go and read the novel itself afterwards – but also potentially disconcerting when it turns out that the second experience is markedly different to the first. For in the nature of things, film 'adaptations' are precisely that: texts which have to do things to the original text in order to become a film (of limited duration) and to attract a modern audience. What interests me, and what I shall briefly explore in this new 'Postscript' to a volume in which I have presented Hardy's fiction as radically subversive in both content and texture, is what kind of 'things' get done to his work by modern film-makers, and what their implications may be for the representation of Hardy as 'our contemporary'.

However, before considering more recent film versions of Hardy's fiction, it is worth noting that there were four silent films made during his own lifetime and one the year after he died: a Famous Players Film Company (USA) version of *Tess of the d'Urbervilles* in 1913; a Turner Films Ltd (UK) *Far from the Madding Crowd* in 1915; a Progress Film Company (UK) *The Mayor of Casterbridge* in 1921; a Metro-Goldwin-Mayer (USA) *Tess* in 1924; and a British International Pictures (UK) *Under the Greenwood Tree* in 1929.[2] Given how recent was the provenance of the new technological art form, it is to Hardy's credit that in his seventies and eighties he could react with considerable aplomb, as his letters reveal, to the overtures made to him to adapt his work for the cinema – perhaps merely confirming the now long-running critical notion that Hardy was, in himself, already a 'filmic' writer who had an instinctive and prescient sympathy with the form. Nevertheless, he was artistically anxious about what would be done to his work when he lost control of it to another medium. Apropos of the 1913 version of *Tess of the d'Urbervilles*, for instance, he wrote that he could see no objection to a film of the novel being made, as long as 'the producers are clearly given to understand that it must be done seriously, and that the story must not be vulgarized or treated lightly, so that all possibility of a farcical view of the tragedy is prevented'.[3] Of the five films mentioned above, however, all prints are, in the words of the movie databases, 'presumed lost'. It is one of 'life's little ironies', therefore – one I am not sure Hardy himself would have savoured – that the only extant silent film version of one of his novels made in his lifetime seems to be D.W. Griffith's *Way Down East* of 1920 (starring Lillian Gish) – a reworking, albeit heavily disguised (it is set in 'contemporary' New England, contains 'farcical' scenes, and has a happy ending), of *Tess of the d'Urbervilles*.[4]

A fallow period followed Hardy's death, lasting until John Schlesinger's film of *Far from the Madding Crowd* in 1967, with a screenplay by Frederic Raphael and starring Julie Christie, Terence Stamp, Peter Finch and Alan Bates. The 1970s saw TV 'mini-series' of *Jude the Obscure* (1971) and *Wessex Tales* (1973), culminating with BBC TV's seven-part adaptation of *The Mayor of Casterbridge* as 'The Classic Serial' (1978; screenplay by Dennis Potter, starring Alan Bates and Anna Massey), and Roman Polanski's feature film, *Tess* (1979; starring Nastassja Kinski, Peter Firth and Leigh Lawson). A TV film version of *The Return of the Native* was broadcast in 1994 (with Catherine Zeta-Jones, Clive Owen, Joan Plowright and Ray Stevenson), while the later 1990s saw Michael Winterbottom's *Jude* (1996; starring Christopher Ecclestone, Kate Winslet and Rachel Griffiths), Phil Agland's *The Woodlanders* (1997; with Emily Woof, Rufus Sewell and Cal Macaninch), Sarah Wilson's TV film of *Tess of the d'Urbervilles* (1998; with Justine Waddell, Jason Flemyng and

Oliver Milburn), and Nicholas Renton's Granada TV film of *Far from the Madding Crowd* (1998; with Paloma Baeza, Nigel Terry, Nathaniel Parker and Jonathan Firth). The films listed here are by no means the only ones to have been made recently, nor should we forget that a film like Michael Winterbottom's *The Claim* (2000) is actually based on *The Mayor of Casterbridge*. What kind of 'Hardy', then, are modern films projecting for us?

A structural irony in Hardy studies at the start of the new millennium is that where contemporary literary criticism is busy recasting his work as radically subversive in form and content, film and TV, the most prevalent and popular late-twentieth-century modes of reproducing it, often seem to return us to an older, more conventional Hardy – of 'Wessex', 'Character and Environment' and humanist tragedy. Apropos, in the mid-1990s, the *Independent on Sunday* while predicting that '1996 would be the year of the Wessex novelist and poet', and quoting the film-makers as finding in Hardy's novels 'essentially modern concerns' (young people thwarted by fate, 'powerful female characters', 'getting an education to better oneself') – nevertheless presented the fiction authoritatively as being about 'man's deepest passions, amid the countryside of Wessex, far from the fashionable concerns of the metropolis'.[5] It is in the apparent contradiction here that we may find the two main discourses traversing 'Hardy on screen': that which sees him as the reliquary of aspects of the English national heritage and himself a constituent of it, thus presenting his work in terms of an authentic, period realism; and that which tries to make him relevant to a thoroughly modern audience. Let me look first and briefly[6] at the earlier major film versions of Hardy's fiction as evincing the duality of focus outlined here.

Partly because of the principal actors – at once their faces and their pre-existing fame as stars of other Sixties' movies (this is especially true of Julie Christie and Terence Stamp) – John Schlesinger's 1967 film of *Far from the Madding Crowd* is indelibly marked as 'modern' (critics at the time constantly remarked on this – one newspaper headline reading: 'What's a swinging 1967 girl doing in Hardy's Dorset?'[7]). Indeed, despite its careful fidelity to period setting and detail, and to the novel in terms of basic plot, character and depiction of rural environment – the photography ceaselessly emphasising the aura of bucolic romance – the film emerges as a form of 1960s pastoral: a bright, exuberant and colourful filmic display (clearly borrowing tropes from Fellini), in which Julie Christie ('sexy', 'radiant', and star of *Darling* the previous year) seems to play an emancipated 1960s young woman, who starts up her own business, has a series of difficult love-affairs, but settles down happily and prosperously in the end. However faithful a factual rendering of the novel and its period the film may be, therefore, its tone and stance, its essentially upbeat Sixties romanticism, tinged occasionally with touches of anxiety, effectively and simultaneously de- and re-historicises Hardy as a participant in the Swinging Decade.

A similar process, but very differently inflected, can be seen in the BBC TV *The Mayor of Casterbridge* of 1978. The film is, in many respects, a superb example of period drama, painstakingly faithful to the novel in plot, dialogue, theme, character and physical description. Indeed, it may be seen as a full-scale modern reproduction of the conventionally conceived 'Thomas Hardy': tragic humanist and rural annalist; the novelist of 'Character and Environment'; the 'Wessex' realist *par excellence* (see Chapters 1 and 2 in the present volume). What is striking about the film is its overriding concern with its own authenticity; or, to put it another way, its meaning *is* its realism, its fidelity to the novel and to a notion of historical period. But in this, what it is really true to is the historical myth of 'Wessex', a fiction of the (English) past. This we might see as 'Environment'; but the film's other predominant focus ('Character as Destiny') is the rise and fall, the individual tragedy of a 'Man of Character', Michael Henchard. The effect of this, however, is to keep the two terms separate: rather than Henchard being seen as engulfed by historical process, we have a personal drama of human character played out against a visually pleasing and authentic, but fictive, period environment. Paradoxically, therefore, the film dehistoricises the novel by fetishising facticity and by envisioning a static relationship between character and its social environment: the Myth of 'Wessex', in other words, replaces the history of Dorset.

Roman Polanski's *Tess* (1979), although we may see in it a further manifestation of the oscillation between period authenticity and modern consciousness, is markedly different to both those discussed above in that it offers a modern *re-interpretation* of the original novel – and of the protagonist in particular. Once again basically faithful to Hardy's novel in plot and dialogue, beautifully photographed, and very long, *Tess* establishes its environments in great depth and density, thus attaining the sense of solid historical realism I have noted in the TV *The Mayor of Casterbridge*. Unlike the latter, however, it is not interested in the past as a museum-piece, but rather as an appropriate period setting for what Polanski called 'a great love story'.[8] Hence, it does not use the historical past, either, to denote a dynamic set of social relations which determine Tess's destiny. In fact, the reverse is the case, for the film, emblematised by its close-ups of Nastassja Kinski's lovely face, is centred very clearly on the character of Tess herself, and it is here that Polanski's interpretative frame becomes most apparent. In an interview in 1979, he said: 'Tess belongs to the present, to the modern age, to you and me. She is the first truly modern heroine'.[9] What this means is that the character, while superimposed on a realistic period background, is not organically related to it; rather, she is figured as existentially alienated from her society. This is done by playing down or excising those parts of the novel which embed Tess very firmly in an historical community (for example, the early scene in which the Durbeyfield horse, Prince, is killed by a mail-cart is cut, thus minimising the sense in which Tess is entrapped by heredity, family, class and social change). Estranged from her age and located in the film primarily in her own emotional space (Kinski plays Tess as constantly in a passive, dreamy, almost trance-like state), the retention of her own personal integrity becomes the film's main message. In this way, Polanski reproduces Tess as someone trying to live an authentic life in an inauthentic society: in fact, as the existential heroine of his own time and tragic vision.

Before I turn to more recent films, I would like to make it clear that in these commentaries, I do not intend to be negatively critical by claiming that the films are 'unfaithful' to the books, nostalgic, sentimental, shallow, trite or anachronistic, nor that modern directors should not interpret the books as any literary critic would. On the contrary, many of the films for the most part follow the plot assiduously, are visually stunning, excellently acted, sensitively interpreted and directed, and quite properly reproduce the novels as 'contemporary' texts – indeed, how could they not? What I *do* claim, however – and perhaps the giveaway here is the phrase 'for the most part' above – is that certain things Hardy's novels do, the films cannot or will not do – especially, the tendency of the former to undermine their own realism, to foreground their disruptive tropes, to burlesque their own tragedies.

Let me take as an example here the 1998 Granada TV version of *Far from the Madding Crowd*. This is a loving, languorous, extremely faithful version of the novel, very much in the spirit of Hardy's first real publishing success, which is also finely acted and beautifully photographed. Of course, as with any film adaptation, things are changed or omitted for cinematic effect: for instance, where the novel lets the reader know at the time that Sergeant Troy has not in fact drowned while swimming in the sea after Fanny's death, the film keeps the viewer in the dark – fair enough, one is tempted to think. But nevertheless, the film does seem to erase those characteristic discourses inscribed in Hardy's text which somehow turn the edge of the surrounding humanist-realist narrative. For example, where we may have no hesitation in noticing how emphatically and ironically the novel contains discourses of scopophilia (especially of the male characters looking at Bathsheba, who identifies herself as 'a watched woman', and of whom the novel says: 'Gabriel's espial had made her an indecorous woman without her own connivance'[10]), the film, in its own lingering visualisation of Bathsheba-Baeza's beautiful young face, does not create the ironic distance on its own discourses that Hardy's text arguably does. Rather, the viewer is forced into collusion with the scopophilic camera, thus failing to be directed back to the male gaze *within* the film, and so being prevented from seeing how Bathsheba is constructed and appropriated by that gaze. Indeed, what is striking is the way the opening scenes of the film omit almost all the opportunities for this.

Such omissions or suppressions are more structurally apparent in Michael Winterbottom's *Jude*. While many of the film's scenes accurately replicate those in *Jude the Obscure*, the plot by and large follows Hardy's, and many of the characters' utterances are more or less verbatim quotations from the book, there is also, as is to be expected, quite a lot changed or missing. But it is more in the *nature* of the changes and absences, rather than in the fact of them, that we can most clearly discern the cultural refashioning of the novel to make it into an acceptable modern film. Let me offer a couple of examples. First, the casting of Kate Winslet as Sue seems to me to have been a mistake: physiognomically, she has an inescapably modern face, that of the untroubled and cossetted commuter-belt maiden she seems to be, which is deeply unconvincing. Whether or not this was the result of the backers wanting to include a contemporary cult actress in the film, or whether it was a strategic attempt to forge an identification between the problems of a nineteenth-century 'New Woman' and those of the (equivocally) emancipated young women of the 1990s, it gives *Jude* a nicer and gentler patina than the novel would suggest. Even more disconcerting is the question of why Arabella's character is altered in the way that it is. From the novel's rough, cunning, lewd woman of 'rank passions', who satirically 'degrades' the tragically earnest story of the main characters, she becomes in the film a sexy but sweet country girl who makes love to Jude with affectionate abandon, and later turns into a contrite and respectable widow who is nice both to Little Father Time and to Jude in his extremity. Domesticating Arabella is no mean achievement, so why do it?

It is the way the film ends, however, that is most striking: where Jude dies at the end of the novel, he does not in the film. What is also missing in the film is the fact that, after Sue returns to Phillotson, the anything but respectable Arabella effectively tricks Jude into remarrying her in scenes of considerable squalor, drunkenness and chicanery, so that Jude is deeply degraded by her before he makes his final futile journey to see Sue at Phillotson's in pouring rain, which is the immediate cause of the illness that results in his death. Not quite the stuff of which period drama is made, one might think, nor of charismatic cult heroes. Furthermore, on the last page of the novel's penultimate chapter, with Jude fatally ill upstairs, Arabella makes up to the quack physician, Vilbert – a character and scene also omitted from the film. Finally, if we remember the last grotesquely ironic chapter of the novel (described on pp. 69–70 of the present volume), we again wonder what possessed the film-makers to end their film as they did. But we also have a clue here. There is surely no way that a modern director making the kind of 'classic drama' film he is making – in association with the BBC – could end his adaptation with a scene in such seemingly absurd bad taste as that which closes *Jude the Obscure*. It would make a mockery of everything that has gone before: of the intense love-story, of its contemporary relevance, of the tragedy of these young lives, but most particularly of the decorum of that authentic tragic realism which the film has so lovingly strived for in acting and setting throughout. The neutralizing of Arabella as a fiercely 'carnivalizing' presence in the novel, together with the changed ending, seem to suggest that Hardy's anti-humanist, anti-realist satirical fiction can only be granted the status of classic tragic realism precisely when all those elements of his text which make such a reading untenable are stripped out or suppressed. The film *Jude*, in other words, had to recast the novel in drastic fashion in order to be able to make an acceptable modern film of it at all.

Similarly with Phil Agland's 1997 film of *The Woodlanders*, hailed by *Esquire* magazine as 'the best film adaptation ever produced from a Thomas Hardy novel'.[11] Once again, it is beautifully filmed in some wonderfully appropriate settings; has some fine acting, especially by Emily Woof who catches exactly Grace's extreme youthfulness and even more stunningly her 'characterlessness' which the novel describes so perversely but pointedly (see p. 57 above); and the 'periodisation' is minutely realistic, as one would expect from a production of this kind. Indeed, the film displays the kind of fetishisation of period which dominates these classic adaptations, so that at times visual authenticity seems to be the *raison d'être* for their being made in the first place. While the main story remains faithful to the book – the class ambitions of Mr Melbury for his daughter, for example, being well understood and enacted – little is made of Hardy's examination of the 'metamorphic' impact in class terms of arrivistes on a rural community itself in transition (see pp. 52 ff., above). But the film also leaves so much out texturally that the polyphony of the novel is restricted to a singular narrative tune – that of Grace and her love affairs. It is noticeable again that the more *outré* elements of the novel are erased: for example, the business of Marty South's father and his obsession with the tree (which Fitzpiers is responsible for having cut down) is entirely omitted, as is (surprisingly) Fitzpiers's roll in the hay with Suke Damson after the midsummer-night rite when he has already 'chosen' Grace as his wife-to-be. Mrs Charmond is reduced from the irresponsible *femme fatale* of 'sensational' fiction (see p. 58) to someone who is rather pathetically in love with Fitzpiers, while the account of her separation from him (re. Marty's hair) and of her melodramatic death is never alluded to (see p. 56); nor, too, is the satirical symbolism of her association with mantraps (see p. 60).

But it is the ending of the film that is once again most striking. In effect, it ends with Chapter 56 of the novel, while the latter goes on to Chapter 58; in the novel, Grace never says she feels 'nothing' for Fitzpiers – rather, and characteristically, under his intense pressure, she is hesitant and diffident in her replies; and the omitted chapters contain all the burlesque doings which are described on p. 56 above: the business of Suke Damson, Tim Tangs and the mantrap; Grace's skirt being fortuitously caught in it; the meeting with Fitzpiers; the chance arrival at 'that newly done-up place, the Earl of Wessex'; the rustics' meditations on women and marriage; Grace's departure to the Midlands with Fitzpiers; Marty's final lament over Giles's grave: "'Now, my own love, ... you are mine, and only mine; for she has forgot 'ee at last, although for her you died, ...'".[12] It is particularly surprising that the film does not close with this last scene, since it is an ending no one ever quite forgets and also one which seems to be eminently filmic.

How, then, might one begin to explain this foreshortening of the novel, along with the other omissions and changes? And what might the 'new' ending of the film version imply? First, as with the film of *Jude*, there is a sense that contemporary 'period' film-makers with a modern audience in mind cannot countenance the mixture of modes which Hardy's novels contain. If you are making/expecting a tragic love-story, then you don't have your wronged heroine getting her skirt (not even her leg) caught in a mantrap laid for her errant husband by the jealous husband of a randy country girl on the eve of their emigration to New Zealand – a hoyden who has committed the act of darkness with said errant husband on the night he was affianced and on sundry occasions since. Nor do you have the wronged heroine a) fortuitously meeting up with errant husband and agreeing to accompany him to the Earl of Wessex pub (her only anxiety being that "'I haven't a brush or comb or anything!" '[13]), where b) by chance her father finds her and she tells him in passing c) that she's been caught in a mantrap, and d) that she's getting back together with errant husband and will accompany him to a large medical practice in the Midlands. Nor again do you close the film with a sweet and faithful country girl claiming for her own the dead love of the heroine in a moody elegy which steals the thunder from the heroine's now heartfelt but thwarted love for the deceased hero. In other words, you can't mix into the tragic love-story elements which continuously undercut its earnest seriousness and introduce 'satires of circumstance' which a modern audience could not comprehend in the context of a realist tragedy. Furthermore, if you end your film with the heroine (and star actress) rejecting forever the errant husband in a firm but feeling manner, implying undying love for dead lover and cool disdain for living husband, you are making a 'right-on' gendered statement about fidelity of a distinctly modern idealistic variety: Grace Melbury Victrix.

What we await, then, rather than consoling period dramas, are film versions of novels by Hardy that can cope with and enact the unstable and destabilising mix of his fictional modes and their pawky satire on relations between the sexes in a 'metamorphic' class society.

Notes

CHAPTER 1. HARDY OUR CONTEMPORARY?

1. Catherine Pepinster, 'From Drawing-Rooms to Wessex Wilds', *Independent on Sunday*, 31 Dec. 1995.
2. Frank Smyth, 'Village Cat Ate Thomas Hardy's Heart', *Observer*, 31 Dec. 1995. Significantly, in the *Sunday Telegraph Magazine* of 26 May 1996, there was also a piece entitled 'Hardy Perennial' – by Adam Nicolson, but supposedly in Thomas Hardy's voice – which complains about the physical desecration of 'Wessex' and the 'imminent vulgarisation' of Hardy's work by film-makers, the 'Heritage' industry, and commercial interests (especially 'The Thomas Hardy Brewery').

CHAPTER 3. HARDY AMONGST THE CRITICS

1. Timothy Hands, *Thomas Hardy* (Writers in their Time; Basingstoke: Macmillan, 1995), p. xii. For a comprehensive selection of early criticism of Hardy's fiction and poetry, see R. G. Cox (ed.), *Thomas Hardy: The Critical Heritage* (2nd edn., London: Routledge & Kegan Paul, 1970).
2. *New Quarterly Review* (Oct. 1879); J. M. Barrie, 'Thomas Hardy: The Historian of Wessex', *Contemporary Review*, 56 (1889); both in Cox (ed.), *Thomas Hardy: The Critical Heritage*, 67, 159.
3. Alfred C. Baugh (ed.), *A Literary History of England* (London: Routledge & Kegan Paul, 1967; 2nd edn. 1970), 1466–8.
4. David Cecil, *Hardy the Novelist* (London: Constable, 1943), 32.
5. Douglas Brown, *Thomas Hardy* (1954; Harlow: Longman, 1961), 31.
6. I am indebted to Charles Swann of Keele University for this quotation.
7. F. R. Leavis, *The Great Tradition* (1948; Harmondsworth: Penguin, 1962), 140.

8. Peter Casagrande, *Unity in Hardy's Novels: 'Repetitive Symmetries'* (Basingstoke: Macmillan, 1982), 11, 223.
9. Joe Fisher, in *The Hidden Hardy* (Basingstoke: Macmillan, 1992), deals interestingly with several of the 'minor novels' (see Ch. 4 for an outline of his approach); and Penny Boumelha has an essay, '"A Complicated Position for Women": *The Hand of Ethelberta*', in Margaret R. Higgonet (ed.), *The Sense of Sex: Feminist Perspectives on Hardy* (Urbana, Ill.: University of Illinois Press, 1993), 242–59.
10. Respectively: unsigned review in *Saturday Review*, 87 (7 Jan. 1899), 19; Chambers's review in *Athenaeum*, 14 Jan. 1899; and unsigned reviews in *Academy*, 23 Nov. 1901, and *Athenaeum*, 4 Jan. 1902; all in J. Gibson and T. Johnson (eds.), *Thomas Hardy: Poems* (Casebooks; Basingstoke: Macmillan, 1979; rev. edn., 1993), 41–2, 43, 44, 46, 52.
11. Pound wrote this in 1937; see *The Letters of Ezra Pound, 1907–1941*, ed. D. D. Paige, (New York: Harcourt, Brace, 1950), 294.
12. F. R. Leavis, *New Bearings in English Poetry* (1932; Harmondsworth: Penguin, 1963), 53, 56.
13. Mark Van Doren, *Autobiography* (New York: Harcourt, Brace, 1958), 167.
14. Donald Davie, *Thomas Hardy and British Poetry* (London: Routledge & Kegan Paul, 1973), 27–9.
15. Samuel Hynes (ed.), *Thomas Hardy: A Critical Selection of his Finest Poetry* (Oxford: Oxford University Press, 1984), Introduction, p. xxi (see later in this chapter for more on this and its 1994 'companion' volume, *Thomas Hardy: A Selection of his Finest Poems* (Oxford: Oxford University Press).
16. Harry Thomas (ed.), *Thomas Hardy: Selected Poems* (Penguin Classics; Harmondsworth: Penguin, 1993), Preface, pp. xi–xii.
17. David Wright (ed.), *Thomas Hardy: Selected Poems* (The Penguin Poetry Library; Harmondsworth: Penguin, 1978; rev. edn., 1986), Introduction, 15–16; 'Note on the Selection', 29.
18. T. R. M. Creighton (ed.), *Poems of Thomas Hardy: A New Selection* (Basingstoke: Macmillan, 1974), Introduction, pp. viii–ix.
19. Andrew Motion (ed.), *Thomas Hardy: Selected Poems* (Everyman; London: Orion, 1994), pp. xxi–xxii.
20. Hynes, *A Critical Selection* (1984), Introduction, pp. xxi, xxii, xxiv; *A Selection*, pp. xiii, xiv, xvii.
21. Obvious examples would include: 'The Darkling Thrush', 'The Oxen', 'An August Midnight', 'Weathers', 'The Convergence of the Twain', 'In Time of "The Breaking of Nations"', 'At Castle Boterel', 'Beeny Cliff', 'The Voice', and others of the 'Poems of 1912–13'. The 'Familiar Hardy' section in Peter Widdowson (ed.), *Thomas Hardy: Selected Poetry and Non-Fictional Prose* (Basingstoke: Macmillan, 1996) contains the eighty or so poems of this kind, and

the critical commentary there discusses in detail the process by which they have become so.

22. U. C. Knoepflmacher, 'Hardy Ruins: Female Spaces and Male Designs', in Higgonet (ed.), *The Sense of Sex*, 107, 109.
23. Quoted in Davie, *Thomas Hardy and British Poetry*, 27.

CHAPTER 4. HARDY THE NOVELIST

1. Terry Coleman, in the Introduction to his edition of Hardy's *An Indiscretion in the Life of an Heiress* (London: Hutchinson, 1976), 5–9, adduces two other 'sources' for our knowledge about it: an article by Hardy's close friend, Sir Edmund Gosse, 'Thomas Hardy's Lost Novel', *Sunday Times*, 22 Jan. 1928; and a letter of 10 Aug. 1868 from Alexander Macmillan to Hardy (in *The Life and Letters of Alexander Macmillan* (London: Macmillan, 1910)) declining publication of this first novel, but praising aspects of it and making detailed comments.
2. Joe Fisher, *The Hidden Hardy* (Basingstoke: Macmillan, 1992, Introduction, esp. 3, 7). I am grateful to Isobel Armstrong for raising with me in the first place the issue of why 'conservative readings' of Hardy's fiction have persisted for so long.
3. *The Collected Letters of Thomas Hardy*, iv. *1909–13*, ed. R. L. Purdy and Michael Millgate (Oxford: Oxford University Press, 1984), 209.
4. Parts of Morley's comments to Macmillan are quoted in *Life*, 58–9. A fuller version is in Robert Gittings, *Young Thomas Hardy* (London: Heinemann, 1975; Harmondsworth: Penguin, 1978), 154.
5. A more extended discussion of the novel appears in my *Hardy in History: A Study in Literary Sociology* (London: Routledge, 1989), ch. 5.
6. Charles Dickens, *Our Mutual Friend* (1864–5; Penguin English Library; Harmondsworth: Penguin, 1971), 48, 52.
7. A fuller analysis will be found in my Introduction to the Everyman edition of the novel (J. M. Dent, forthcoming).
8. Richard H. Taylor, *The Neglected Hardy: Thomas Hardy's Lesser Novels* (Basingstoke: Macmillan, 1982), 112.
9. *Life*, 52, makes it emphatically clear that, as a young man in London in the 1860s, Hardy studied paintings with keen interest. It seems likely, then, that he would at the very least have known about such an infamous contemporary work.
10. A more extended discussion of this is included in my Introduction to *Tess of the d'Urbervilles* (New Casebooks; Basingstoke: Macmillan, 1993).
11. Quoted in 'Note on the Text', *WB* 215.
12. Parts of the 1892 serial version appear as an appendix, *WB* 216 ff.

13. Ibid. 248.
14. Introduction, ibid. 14–15.
15. Ibid. 13, 16–18, 16, 14.

CHAPTER 5. HARDY THE POET

1. Samuel Hynes (ed.), *Thomas Hardy: A Critical Selection of his Finest Poetry* (Oxford: Oxford University Press, 1984), p. xxix; *Thomas Hardy: A Selection of his Finest Poems* (Oxford: Oxford University Press, 1994), p. xxii.
2. e.g. in *Beloved* (1987; New York: Plume Books, 1988), 35, 99, 191.
3. Quoted in T. R. M. Creighton (ed.), *Poems of Thomas Hardy: A New Selection* (Basingstoke: Macmillan, 1974), 335.
4. Tim Armstrong, in his edition, *Thomas Hardy: Selected Poems* (Longman Annotated Texts; Harlow: Longman, 1993), 228, cites Harold Bloom and Tom Paulin as believing this.
5. Hardy's phrase, in the prefatory 'Apology' to *LLE*.
6. Donald Davie, *Thomas Hardy and British Poetry* (London: Routledge & Kegan Paul, 1973), 40, 7, 11, 26.
7. Trevor Johnson, for example, in *A Critical Introduction to the Poems of Thomas Hardy* (Basingstoke: Macmillan, 1991), 181, while noting 'a certain ambiguity about the subject of the poem', states: 'it is not quite clear whether Hardy is addressing Love or the woman he once loved'. I would suggest that it is not Hardy who is doing the 'addressing' at all. John Lucas, in an unpublished paper, also sees the poem as Hardy remembering a lost love – and will not accept that my reading is the more accurate one!
8. See the poem 'Faintheart in a Railway Train', *LLE*; for 'lost prize', see 'Thoughts of Phena', *WP*.

CHAPTER 7. POSTSCRIPT

1. Books are also now being published on the subject. For example, Paul J. Niemeyer, *Seeing Hardy: Film and Television Adaptations of the Fiction of Thomas Hardy* (Jefferson, N. Carolina and London: MacFarlane, 2003), and Terence Wright (ed.), *Thomas Hardy on Screen* (Cambridge: Cambridge University Press, 2005).
2. Full details of all these films will be found in Appendix A of Niemeyer, op. cit., and in the Filmography in Wright (ed.), op. cit.
3. Richard Little Purdy and Michael Millgate (eds.), *The Collected Letters of Thomas Hardy*, 7 vols (Oxford: Clarendon Press, 1984), vol. IV, 265.

4. See my essay, 'The Silent Era: Thomas Hardy Goes Way Down East', in Wright (ed.), op. cit.
5. Catherine Pepinster, 'From Drawing-Rooms to Wessex Wilds', *Independent on Sunday*, 31 December 1995.
6. As my Acknowledgements make clear, I have written more extensively elsewhere about film versions of Hardy's fiction.
7. Title of a piece by Alexander Walker in the *Evening Standard*, 19 October, 1967.
8. Columbia Press Release (in British Film Institute archive), 5.
9. Harlan Kennedy, '*Tess*: Polanski in Hardy Country', *American Film*, 5, 1 (October 1979), 65.
10. Thomas Hardy, *Far From the Madding Crowd* (1874), ed. by R. Morgan with S. L. Russell. (Penguin Classics. London: Penguin Books, 2000), 311, 18.
11. Quoted on the video cassette box.
12. Thomas Hardy, *The Woodlanders* (1887), ed. by P. Ingham. (Penguin Classics. London: Penguin Books, 1998), 367.
13. Ibid., 359.

Select Bibliography

WORKS BY THOMAS HARDY

Collected Editions

The standard complete edition of all Hardy's works – for the most part prepared for publication by the author – is the Wessex Edition in 24 volumes (London: Macmillan, 1912–31). Hardy's *Collected Poems* was first published in 1919, and revised in 1923, 1928, and 1930. The last two editions form the basis for James Gibson (ed.), *Thomas Hardy: The Complete Poems* (New Wessex edn.; Basingstoke: Macmillan, 1976), which is also the text for Gibson's *Variorum* edition (Macmillan, 1979). However, the most comprehensive collected edition is now Samuel Hynes (ed.), *The Complete Poetical Works of Thomas Hardy* (5 vols.; Oxford: Oxford University Press, 1982, 1984, 1985, 1995) (the final two volumes contain Hardy's epic verse-drama, *The Dynasts*, and his play, *The Famous Tragedy of the Queen of Cornwall*, together with other dramatic pieces).

The following editions of individual novels and selections of poetry are either the ones referred to in the present volume or are recommended as alternative modern texts.

Fiction

The novels are listed in order of their first publication, but are all in the Macmillan New Wessex edition, originally of 1974–5. Publication details, therefore, are not repeated in full for each individual volume. This edition has been reprinted on a number of occasions (sometimes with different covers), and was reissued with new typography in 1985.

Desperate Remedies (1871), with intro, by C. J. P. Beatty (1975).
Under the Greenwood Tree (1872), with intro, by Geoffrey Grigson (1974).
A Pair of Blue Eyes (1873), with intro. by Ronald Blythe (1975).

Far from the Madding Crowd (1874), with intro, by James Gibson (1974/5).
The Hand of Ethelberta (1876), with intro, by Robert Gittings (1975).
The Return of the Native (1878), with intro, by J. C. S. Tremblett-Wood (1974/5).
The Trumpet-Major (1880), with intro, by Ray Evans (1974/5).
A Laodicean (1881), with intro. by Barbara Hardy (1975).
Two on a Tower (1882), with intro, by F. B. Pinion (1975).
The Mayor of Casterbridge (1886), with intro. by F. B. Pinion (1974/5).
The Woodlanders (1887), with intro, by F. B. Pinion (1974/5).
Tess of the d'Urbervilles (1891), with intro. by James Gibson (1974/5).
Jude the Obscure (1896), with intro, by Terry Eagleton (1974).
The Well-Beloved (1897), with intro. by J. Hillis Miller (1975).

Good modern editions of many of Hardy's novels are also available in The Penguin Classics and OUP's The World's Classics series.

Hardy's short stories were collected and published in four volumes: *Wessex Tales* (1888), *A Group of Noble Dames* (1891), *Life's Little Ironies* (1894), and *A Changed Man and Other Tales* (1913). The first of these is reprinted in the New Wessex edition (with intro. by F. B. Pinion (1976, 1986)), in The World's Classics (ed. Kathryn R. King (Oxford University Press, 1991)), in 'Wordsworth Classics' (1995), and by Longman (ed. Robert Southwick (1995)); the third is in The World's Classics (ed. Alan Manford and Norman Page (Oxford University Press, 1996)); and all four are reprinted by the Folio Society (1987, 1994). *The Collected Short Stories*, with intro. by Desmond Hawkins, is in the New Wessex edition (in 3 vols., 1977; in 1 vol., 1988), and selections are also published in the New Wessex, Penguin English Library, Everyman Paperbacks, and Macmillan Student's Hardy series.

Poetry

The following selections are either currently in print or are relatively recent editions referred to in the course of the present volume.

Armstrong, Tim (ed.), *Thomas Hardy: Selected Poems* (Longman Annotated Texts; Harlow: Longman, 1993).
Creighton, T. R. M., (ed.), *Poems of Thomas Hardy: A New Selection* (Basingstoke: Macmillan, 1974).
Hynes, Samuel (ed.), Thomas Hardy: *A Critical Selection of his Finest Poetry* (The Oxford Authors; Oxford: Oxford University Press, 1984).
——— (ed.) *Thomas Hardy: A Selection of his Finest Poems* (Oxford Poetry Library; Oxford: Oxford University Press, 1994).
Motion, Andrew (ed.), *Thomas Hardy: Selected Poems* (Everyman; London: Orion, 1994).

Orel, Harold (ed.), *The Dynasts* (New Wessex series; Basingstoke: Macmillan, 1978).

Thomas, Harry (ed.), *Thomas Hardy. Selected Poems* (Penguin Classics; Harmondsworth: Penguin, 1993).

Wain, John (ed.), *Selected Shorter Poems of Thomas Hardy* (Basingstoke: Macmillan, 1966; rev. edn., 1975).

——— and Wain, Eirian (eds.), *The New Wessex Selection of Thomas Hardy's Poetry* (Basingstoke: Macmillan, 1978).

Widdowson, Peter (ed.), *Thomas Hardy: Selected Poetry and Non-Fictional Prose* (Basingstoke: Macmillan, 1996).

Willmott, Richard (ed.), *Thomas Hardy: Selected Poems* (Oxford Student Texts; Oxford: Oxford University Press, 1992).

Wright, David (ed.), *Thomas Hardy: Selected Poems* (The Penguin Poetry Library; Harmondsworth: Penguin, 1978; rev. edn., 1986).

Miscellaneous works

Björk, Lennart (ed.), *The Literary Notebooks of Thomas Hardy* (2 vols.; Basingstoke: Macmillan, 1985).

Greenslade, William (ed.), *Thomas Hardy's 'Facts' Notebook. a Critical Edition* (Aldershot: Ashgate, 2004).

Thomas Hardy, *An Indiscretion in the Life of an Heiress*, ed., with an introduction, Terry Coleman (London: Hutchinson, 1976).

———*An Indiscretion in the Life of an Heiress*, ed., with an introduction, Pamela Daiziel (World's Classics; Oxford: Oxford University Press, 1994).

Orel, Harold (ed.), *Thomas Hardy's Personal Writings* (Basingstoke: Macmillan, 1966; rev, edn., 1990).

Purdy, Richard, and Millgate, Michael (eds.), *The Collected Letters of Thomas Hardy* (7 vols.; Oxford: Oxford University Press, 1978–88). (Millgate has also edited *Selected Letters* (Oxford: Oxford University Press, 1990.))

Taylor, Richard H. (ed.), *The Personal Notebooks of Thomas Hardy* (Basingstoke: Macmillan, 1978).

BIBLIOGRAPHIES

Draper, R. P., and Ray, M., *An Annotated Critical Bibliography of Thomas Hardy* (London: Harvester Wheatsheaf, 1989). Selective summary of major books and articles about him.

Gerber, H., and Davis, E., *Thomas Hardy: An Annotated Bibliography of Writings about Him* (2 vols.; Urbana, Ill.: University of Illinois Press, 1973, 1983).

Purdy, R. L., *Thomas Hardy: A Bibliographical Study* (Oxford: Oxford University Press, 1954). The standard work.

BIOGRAPHIES

Gibson, James, *Thomas Hardy: A Literary Life* (Basingstoke: Macmillan, 1996).

Gittings, Robert, *Young Thomas Hardy* (London: Heinemann, 1975; Harmondsworth: Penguin, 1978).

——— *The Older Hardy* (London: Heinemann, 1978).

Hardy, Florence Emily, *The Life of Thomas Hardy, 1840–1928* (Basingstoke: Macmillan, 1962; paperback edn., 1975) – the one-volume edition of *The Early Life of Thomas Hardy, 1840–1891* (Macmillan, 1928), and *The Later Years of Thomas Hardy, 1892–1928* (Macmillan, 1930), now known to have been largely composed by Hardy himself, with Florence Emily's assistance, during the 1920s. This work has been republished as *The Life and Work of Thomas Hardy* (ed. Michael Millgate (Macmillan, 1985)) – a theoretically 'restored' version of the 'original', before its editing by Florence Emily and Hardy's other executors.

Millgate, Michael, *Thomas Hardy: A Biography* (Oxford: Oxford University Press, 1982; reissued, 1985, 1992).

Seymour-Smith, Martin, *Hardy* (London: Bloomsbury, 1994).

COMPANIONS AND REFERENCE BOOKS

Bailey, J. O., *The Poems of Thomas Hardy: A Handbook and Commentary* (Chapel Hill, NC: University of North Carolina Press, 1970). Standard reference work.

Cox, R. G. (ed.), *Thomas Hardy: The Critical Heritage* (London: Routledge & Kegan Paul, 1970). Contains early reviews and critical essays on poems and novels.

Harvey, Geoffrey, *The Complete Critical Guide to Thomas Hardy* (London: Routledge, 2002).

Kay-Robinson, Denys, *Hardy's Wessex Re-appraised* (Newton Abbot: David & Charles, 1972). Painstaking identification of the 'real' places in Hardy's fiction and poetry.

Kramer, Dale (ed.), *The Cambridge Companion to Thomas Hardy* (Cambridge: Cambridge University Press, (1999).

Page, Norman (ed.), *Oxford Reader's Companion to Hardy* (Oxford: Oxford University Press, 2000).

Pinion, F. B., *A Commentary on the Poems of Thomas Hardy* (Basingstoke: Macmillan, 1975). Standard reference work.

—— *A Hardy Companion* (Basingstoke: Macmillan, 1968; rev. edn., 1978). Standard reference work for all Hardy's writings, especially their geography.

—— *A Thomas Hardy Dictionary* (Basingstoke: Macmillan 1989; rev. edn., 1992). Supplements preceding works in useful alphabetical format.

CRITICAL STUDIES

The works listed below – mainly books, with a smattering of essays and articles – comprise a selection of what I consider to be significant critical contributions to the vast field of Hardy studies. With the odd exception, they all date from the last four decades – when the modern Hardy critical industry really got into gear – and most receive at least passing mention in the body of my text. Many different positions are represented here, but I have attempted to give greater prominence to more contemporary and redirectional perspectives, not because newer means better but to indicate the current complexion of Hardy criticism. Readers are asked to turn to Chapter 3 for a more extended survey of its history and major features. In the list below, I have not offered a view on the worth of the works cited.

Abbott, Rob and Bell, Charlie, *Hardy: a Beginner's Guide* (London: Hodder and Stoughton, 2000–1).

Bayley, John, *An Essay on Hardy* (Cambridge: Cambridge University Press, 1978).

Blake, Kathleen, 'Pure Tess: Hardy on Knowing a Woman', *Studies in English Literature*, 22/4 (Autumn 1982), 689–705.

Boumelha, Penny, *Thomas Hardy and Women: Sexual Ideology and Narrative Form* (Brighton: Harvester Press, 1982).

——(ed.), *Jude the Obscure* (New Casebooks; Basingstoke: Macmillan, 1996).

Brooks, Jean, *Thomas Hardy: The Poetic Structure* (London: Elek Books, 1971).

Bullen, J. B., *The Expressive Eye: Fiction and Perception in the Work of Thomas Hardy* (Oxford: Oxford University Press, 1986).

Casagrande, Peter, *Unity in Hardy's Novels: 'Repetitive Symmetries'* (Basingstoke: Macmillan, 1982).

Davie, Donald, 'Hardy's Virgilian Purples', *Agenda*, 10/2–3 (1972), 138–56.

——— *Thomas Hardy and British Poetry* (London: Routledge & Kegan Paul, 1973).

———*With the Grain: Essays on Thomas Hardy and British Poetry*, ed. and intro. by Clive Wilmer (Manchester; Carcanet, 1998).

Dolin, Tim and Widdowson, Peter, (eds.), *Thomas Hardy and Contemporary Literary Studies* (Basingstoke: Palgrave Macmillan, 2004).

Draper, R. P. (ed.), *Thomas Hardy: The Tragic Novels* (Casebooks; Basingstoke: Macmillan, 1975; rev. edn., 1991). Contains well-known earlier essays by, *inter alia*, Virginia Woolf, Raymond Williams, David Lodge, and Tony Tanner.

Eagleton, Terry, *Criticism and Ideology* (London: Verso, 1978). See brief comments in Chapter 4; also Eagleton's introduction to the New Wessex edition of *Jude the Obscure*.

Fisher, Joe, *The Hidden Hardy* (Basingstoke: Macmillan, 1992).

Garson, Marjorie, *Hardy's Fables of Integrity: Woman, Body, Text* (Oxford: Oxford University Press, 1991).

Gibson, J., and Johnson, T. (eds.), *Thomas Hardy: Poems* (Basingstoke: Macmillan 1979; rev. edn., 1991). Contains selected early reviews of Hardy's volumes of poetry, plus essays by, *inter alia*, Samuel Hynes, Philip Larkin, Thom Gunn, and Frank Giodano.

Goode, John, *Thomas Hardy: The Offensive Truth* (Oxford: Blackwell, 1988).

Gregor, Ian, *The Great Web: The Form of Hardy's Major Fiction* (London: Faber, 1974).

Hands, Timothy, *Thomas Hardy* (Writers in their Time; Basingstoke: Macmillan, 1995). On fiction and poetry.

Hardy, Barbara, *Imagining Imagination: Hardy's Poetry and Fiction* (London: Athlone Press, 2000).

Higgonet, Margaret R. (ed.), *The Sense of Sex: Feminist Perspectives on Hardy* (Urbana, Ill.: University of Illinois Press, 1993). Contains essays by, *inter alia*, Judith Mitchell, Penny Boumelha (on *Ethelberta*), and U. C. Knoepflmacher (on poems).

Hillis Miller, J., *Thomas Hardy: Distance and Desire* (Oxford: Oxford University Press, 1970).

———*Fiction and Repetition: Seven English Novels* (Cambridge, Mass.: Harvard University Press, 1982). Contains a chapter on *Tess*.

———*The Linguistic Moment: From Wordsworth to Stevens* (Princeton: Princeton University Press, 1985). Contains an essay on Hardy's poetry.

———*Tropes, Parables, Performatives: Essays on Twentieth-Century Literature* (Hemel Hempstead: Harvester Wheatsheaf, 1990). Further essays on Hardy's poetry.

Hynes, Samuel, *The Pattern of Hardy's Poetry* (Chapel Hill, NC: University of North Carolina Press, 1961).

Ingham, Patricia, *Thomas Hardy: A Feminist Reading* (Hemel Hempstead: Harvester Wheatsheaf, 1989).

Jacobus, Mary, 'Tess: The Making of a Pure Woman', in Susan Lipshitz (ed.), *Tearing the Veil: Essays on Feminity* (London: Routledge & Kegan Paul, 1978).

——— 'Hardy's Magian Retrospect', *Essays in Criticism*, 32 (1982), 258–82. On poems.

Johnson, Trevor, '"Pre-Critical Innocence" and the Anthologist's Hardy', *Victorian Poetry*, 17 (1979), 9–24.

———*A Critical Introduction to the Poems of Thomas Hardy* (Basingstoke: Macmillan, 1991).

Langbaum, Robert, *Thomas Hardy in Our Time* (Basingstoke: Macmillan, 1995). On fiction and poetry.

Larkin, Philip, 'Wanted: Good Hardy Critic' (1966), in *Required Writing: Miscellaneous Pieces, 1955–1982* (London: Faber, 1983).

Leavis, F. R., *New Bearings in English Poetry* (1932; Harmondsworth: Penguin, 1963). See brief comments in Chapter 3 of the present volume.

Lucas, John, *Modern English Poetry from Hardy to Hughes* (London: Batsford, 1986).

Mallett, Philip (ed.), *The Achievement of Thomas Hardy* (Basingstoke: Macmillan, 2000).

———(ed.), *Thomas Hardy: Texts and Contexts* (Basingstoke: Macmillan, 2002).

———(ed.), *Palgrave Advances in Thomas Hardy Studies* (Basingstoke: Palgrave Macmillan, 2004).

Morgan, Rosemary, *Women and Sexuality in the Novels of Thomas Hardy* (London: Routledge, 1988).

Niemeyer, Paul J., *Seeing Hardy: Film and Television Adaptations of the Fiction of Thomas Hardy* (Jefferson, N. Carolina and London: MacFarlane, 2003).

Paulin, Tom, *Thomas Hardy: The Poetry of Perception* (Basingstoke: Macmillan, 1975).

Pinion, F. B., *Thomas Hardy: Art and Thought* (Basingstoke: Macmillan, 1977).

Smith, Stan, *Inviolable Voice: History and Twentieth-Century Poetry* (Dublin: Gill & Macmillan, 1982). See Chapter 2 on Hardy.

Stubbs, Patricia, *Women and Fiction: Feminism and the Novel 1880–1920* (1979; London: Methuen, 1981). See Chapter 4 on Hardy.

Taylor, Dennis, *Hardy's Poetry, 1860–1928* (1981: Basingstoke: Macmillan, 1989).

——— *Hardy's Metres and Victorian Prosody* (Oxford: Oxford University Press, 1988).

Taylor, Richard H., *The Neglected Hardy: Thomas Hardy's Lesser Novels*

(Basingstoke: Macmillan, 1982).
Thomas, Edward, *Edward Thomas on Thomas Hardy*, collected, edited and introduced by Trevor Johnson (Cheltenham: The Cyder Press, 2002).
Vigar, Penelope, *The Novels of Thomas Hardy: Illusion and Reality* (London: Athlone Press, 1974).
Widdowson, Peter, *Hardy in History: A Study in Literary Sociology* (London: Routledge, 1989).
——— (ed.), *Tess of the d'Urbervilles* (New Casebooks; Basingstoke: Macmillan, 1993).
——— *On Thomas Hardy: Late Essays and Earlier* (Basingstoke: Macmillan, 1998).
Williams, Merryn, *Thomas Hardy and Rural England* (Basingstoke: Macmillan, 1972).
——— *A Preface to Hardy* (1976; Harlow: Longman, 1993). On fiction and poetry.
Williams, Raymond, *The English Novel from Dickens to Lawrence* (1970; St Albans: Paladin, 1974). See Chapter 4 (most of this reappears in *The Country and the City* (1973), ch. 18). Other of Williams's comments on Hardy will be found in *Politics and Letters* (1979), sect. IV, ch. 2.
——— and Williams, Merryn, 'Hardy and Social Class', in Norman Page (ed.), *Thomas Hardy: The Writer and His Background* (London: Bell & Hyman, 1980).
Wotton, George, *Thomas Hardy: Towards a Materialist Criticism* (Dublin: Gill & Macmillan, 1985).
Wright, Terence (ed.), *Thomas Hardy on Screen* (Cambridge: Cambridge University Press, 2005).
Zietlow, Paul, *Moments of Vision: The Poetry of Thomas Hardy* (Cambridge, Mass: Harvard University Press, 1974).

INTERNET SOURCES

Rather than listing the very large number of websites now devoted, or making substantial reference, to Hardy, I include the internet address of the 'Hardy on the Web, 1999–2004' 'Links to Useful Websites' page (updated to April 2005) of the Thomas Hardy Association. Most of the listed sites also have a 'Site Evaluation' attached:

http://www.yale.edu/hardysoc/Links/linksone/links_to_hardy.htm

Index

WRITERS AND THEIR WORK

". . . this series promises to outshine its own obviously high reputation."
Times Higher Education Supplement

". . . will build into a fine multi-volume critical encyclopaedia of English literature."
Library Review & Reference Review

". . . Excellent, informative, readable, and recommended."
NATE News

"written by outstanding contemporary critics, whose expertise is flavoured by unashamed enthusiasm for their subjects and the series' diverse aspirations."
Times Educational Supplement

"A useful and timely addition to the ranks of the lit crit and reviews genre. Written in an accessible and authoritative style."
Library Association Record

WRITERS AND THEIR WORK

Title	Author
Alfred Tennyson	*Seamus Perry*
Anita Desai	*Elaine Yee Lin Ho*
Anthony Trollope	*Andrew Sanders*
Byron	*Drummond Bone*
C.S. Lewis	*William Gray*
Charles Dickens	*Rod Mengham*
Chinua Achebe	*Nahem Yousaf*
D.H. Lawrence	*Linda Ruth Williams*
E.M. Forster	*Nicholas Royle*
Franz Kafka	*Michael Wood*
George Eliot	*Josephine McDonagh*
George Orwell	*Douglas Kerr*
Gerard Manley Hopkins	*Daniel Brown*
Harold Pinter	*Mark Taylor-Batty*
Henrik Ibsen, 2nd edition	*Sally Ledger*
Henry James—The Later Writing	*Barbara Hardy*
Jane Austen	*Robert Miles*
John Keats	*Kelvin Everest*
Joseph Conrad	*Cedric Watts*
Leo Tolstoy	*John Bayley*
Oscar Wilde	*Alexandra Warwick*
Paul Scott	*Jacqueline Banerjee*
Percy Bysshe Shelley	*Paul Hamilton*
Philip Larkin, 2nd Edition	*Laurence Lerner*
Robert Browning	*John Woolford*
Rudyard Kipling	*Jan Montefiore*
Samuel Beckett	*Sinéad Mooney*

WRITERS AND THEIR WORK

Title	Author
Samuel Taylor Coleridge	*Stephen Bygrave*
Shashi Deshpande	*Amrita Bhalla*
Sir Walter Scott	*Harriet Harvey Wood*
Stephen Crane	*Kevin J. Hayes*
Swinburne	*Catherine Maxwell*
Sylvia Plath, 2nd edition	*Elisabeth Bronfen*
T.S. Eliot	*Colin MacCabe*
Ted Hughes	*Susan Bassnett*
Thomas Hardy, 2nd Edition	*Peter Widdowson*
V.S. Naipaul	*Suman Gupta*
Victorian Quest Romance	*Robert Fraser*
Virginia Woolf, 2nd Edition	*Laura Marcus*
W.B. Yeasts	*Edward Larrissy*
William Blake	*Steve Vine*
William Golding, 2nd Edition	*Kevin McCarron*
William Makepeace Thackeray	*Richard Salmon*
Wole Soyinka	*Mpalive-Hangson Msiska*